"... ... ... nething very close to magic: the books take ordinary—even banal—objects and animate them with a rich history of invention, political struggle, science, and popular mythology. Filled with fascinating details and conveyed in sharp, accessible prose, the books make the everyday world come to life. Be warned: once you've read a few of these, you'll start walking around your house, picking up random objects, and musing aloud: 'I wonder what the story is behind this thing?'"

Steven Johnson, author of *Where Good Ideas Come From* and *How We Got to Now*

"Object Lessons describes themselves as 'short, beautiful books,' and to that, I'll say, amen. . . . If you read enough Object Lessons books, you'll fill your head with plenty of trivia to amaze and annoy your friends and loved ones— caution recommended on pontificating on the objects surrounding you. More importantly, though . . . they inspire us to take a second look at parts of the everyday that we've taken for granted. These are not so much lessons about the objects themselves, but opportunities for self-reflection and storytelling. They remind us that we are surrounded by a wondrous world, as long as we care to look."

John Warner, *The Chicago Tribune*

"In 1957 the French critic and semiotician Roland Barthes published *Mythologies*, a groundbreaking series of essays in which he analysed the popular culture of his day, from laundry detergent to the face of Greta Garbo, professional wrestling to the Citroën DS. This series of short books, Object Lessons, continues the tradition."

Melissa Harrison, *Financial Times*

"Though short, at roughly 25,000 words apiece, these books are anything but slight."

Marina Benjamin, *New Statesman*

"The Object Lessons project, edited by game theory legend Ian Bogost and cultural studies academic Christopher Schaberg, commissions short essays and small, beautiful books about everyday objects from shipping containers to toast. *The Atlantic* hosts a collection of 'mini object-lessons'. . . . More substantive is Bloomsbury's collection of small, gorgeously designed books that delve into their subjects in much more depth."

Cory Doctorow, *Boing Boing*

"The joy of the series ... lies in encountering the various turns through which each of the authors has been put by his or her object. The object predominates, sits squarely center stage, directs the action. The object decides the genre, the chronology, and the limits of the study. Accordingly, the author has to take her cue from the *thing* she chose or that chose her. The result is a wonderfully uneven series of books, each one a *thing* unto itself."

Julian Yates, *Los Angeles Review of Books*

"... edifying and entertaining ... perfect for slipping in a pocket and pulling out when life is on hold."

Sarah Murdoch, *Toronto Star*

"... a sensibility somewhere between Roland Barthes and Wes Anderson."

Simon Reynolds, author of *Retromania: Pop Culture's Addiction to Its Own Past*

OBJECTLESSONS

A book series about the hidden lives of ordinary things.

Series Editors:

Ian Bogost and Christopher Schaberg

Advisory Board:

In association with

LOYOLA UNIVERSITY NEW ORLEANS   Georgia Tech | Center for Media Studies

BOOKS IN THE SERIES

Remote Control by Caetlin Benson-Allott

Golf Ball by Harry Brown

Driver's License by Meredith Castile

Drone by Adam Rothstein

Silence by John Biguenet

Glass by John Garrison

Phone Booth by Ariana Kelly

Refrigerator by Jonathan Rees

Waste by Brian Thill

Hotel by Joanna Walsh

Hood by Alison Kinney

Dust by Michael Marder

Shipping Container by Craig Martin

Cigarette Lighter by Jack Pendarvis

Bookshelf by Lydia Pyne

Password by Martin Paul Eve

Questionnaire by Evan Kindley

Hair by Scott Lowe

Bread by Scott Cutler Shershow

Tree by Matthew Battles

Earth by Jeffrey Jerome Cohen and Linda T. Elkins-Tanton

Traffic by Paul Josephson

Egg by Nicole Walker

Sock by Kim Adrian

Eye Chart by William Germano

Whale Song by Margret Grebowicz

Tumor by Anna Leahy

Jet Lag by Christopher J. Lee

Shopping Mall by Matthew Newton

Personal Stereo by Rebecca Tuhus-Dubrow

Veil by Rafia Zakaria

Burger by Carol J. Adams

Luggage by Susan Harlan

Souvenir by Rolf Potts

Rust by Jean-Michel Rabaté

Doctor by Andrew Bomback

Fake by Kati Stevens

Blanket by Kara Thompson

High Heel by Summer Brennan

Pill by Robert Bennett

Potato by Rebecca Earle

Hashtag by Elizabeth Losh (forthcoming)

Train by A. N. Devers (forthcoming)

Fog by Stephen Sparks (forthcoming)

Wheelchair by Christopher R Smit (forthcoming)

shopping mall

MATTHEW NEWTON

BLOOMSBURY ACADEMIC
NEW YORK · LONDON · OXFORD · NEW DELHI · SYDNEY

BLOOMSBURY ACADEMIC
Bloomsbury Publishing Inc
1385 Broadway, New York, NY 10018, USA
50 Bedford Square, London, WC1B 3DP, UK

BLOOMSBURY, BLOOMSBURY ACADEMIC and the Diana logo are trademarks of
Bloomsbury Publishing Plc

First published 2017
Reprinted 2019 (twice), 2020

Cover design: Alice Marwick

Library of Congress Cataloging-in-Publication Data
Names: Newton, Matthew, 1977 Jan. 06- author.
Title: Shopping mall / Matthew Newton.
Description: New York : Bloomsbury Academic, 2017. | Series: Object lessons |
Includes bibliographical references and index.
Identifiers: LCCN 2017007492| ISBN 9781501314827 (paperback) | ISBN
9781501314834 (epdf)
Subjects: LCSH: Shopping malls—United States—History. | Newton, Matthew,
1977 Jan. 06- | BISAC: LITERARY CRITICISM / Semiotics & Theory. |
PHILOSOPHY / Aesthetics. | SOCIAL SCIENCE / Media Studies.
Classification: LCC HF5430.3 .N49 2017 | DDC 381/.110973—dc23
LC record available at https://lccn.loc.gov/2017007492

ISBN: PB: 978-1-5013-1482-7
ePDF: 978-1-5013-1483-4
ePub: 978-1-5013-1481-0

Series: Object Lessons

Typeset by Deanta Global Publishing Services, Chennai, India
Printed and bound in Great Britain

To find out more about our authors and books visit www.bloomsbury.com
and sign up for our newsletters.

For Michelle, Ethan, anc Nico.

CONTENTS

Prologue 1

PART ONE CHILDHOOD 23

1 Eternal spring 25

2 Paradise unknown 37

3 Spaces between 49

4 Shopping is a feeling 57

PART TWO ADOLESCENCE 63

5 Little boxes 65

6 White denim 70

7 Mall madness 78

8   Neon hallways 88

9   Young love 103

PART THREE **ADULTHOOD** 111

10   Homecoming 113

11   Ghost malls 119

12   Utopia interrupted 127

13   New futures 135

Acknowledgments 143
Notes 144
Index 149

PROLOGUE

A place on a map is also a place in history.
—ADRIENNE RICH, *BLOOD, BREAD, AND POETRY*

"This mall is old," Amiin said through a strong Somali accent. "Been here a long time." When the taxi slowed to a halt outside the food court at Southdale Center in the suburb of Edina, Minnesota, Amiin totaled my fare. I watched his fingers press the buttons on the meter of his minivan taxi. In the near distance, through the rain-dotted windshield, shoppers streamed in and out of the mall's automatic doors, their bodies growing increasingly indistinct between each slow pass of the wiper blades.

It was an early Friday evening in late May, rush hour traffic still heavy on the highways. I had never visited Edina before, let alone Minneapolis. I assessed my surroundings the way you do when you go on vacation and imagine what it might be like to live in that town—how your neighbors and co-workers might talk, what your children's classmates might look like, how the cold air might feel in your lungs on winter mornings when your breath turns to fog.

As Amiin coaxed the meter's slow-moving receipt printer, the alternate life I was imagining faded into what I saw outside. People were coming and going from the mall in a hurry. There were men dressed in khaki pants and Oxford shirts briskly walking past teenagers huddled tight, whispering secrets. There were small groups of Muslim women in hijabs carrying shopping bags. There were silver-haired couples walking arm in arm toward the parking lot. There were ruddy-faced toddlers being pushed in strollers by sleep-deprived parents, their faces illuminated by the glowing screens of their phones. The scenes were familiar yet new; variants of scenarios I had witnessed before, even at other malls, but with different faces, sounds, and landmarks. While this was Edina, it could have been any affluent suburb in America—from New Jersey to Illinois, Texas to California. It was somewhere and nowhere all at once, the type of landscape so familiar that it almost supplants memory, blurring the line between past and present, fiction and reality.

For as long as I can remember, shopping malls have had a strangely calming effect on me. Each visit feels almost like slipping off into a dream—my body taking over as if on autopilot, trusting well-worn neural pathways as a guide. Not only is the mall a place of material reward, it is also a space to meditate on your surroundings. As a child I was shy; the mall was a place to be social at a safe remove. By the time I was a self-conscious teenager, the mall offered invisibility in public—a place to get out of my head but still go unnoticed. As an adult, it is a way back to simpler times; when accessing joy was easier, when life was less burdened. In that way, a shopping mall's banal appearance is perhaps its greatest gift. It offers a blank slate onto which shoppers can project their individual or collective aspirations. Some view it as a place where economic status is celebrated. Others see a mall and its objects as a dream yet—or never—to be attained.

"Here you go, buddy," Amiin said, handing me a ballpoint pen and my receipt attached to a small clipboard. "Need you to sign the bottom."

On our way to the mall, Amiin quizzed me about why I had traveled to Minneapolis. He asked what hotel I was staying at, what type of work I did, and if I had met anyone else who might need a ride. He was doing his job, making small talk while fishing for prospective fares. But when our conversation shifted to his life, it became far more compelling. He told me he had come to the United States from Somalia fifteen years earlier, as a young adult. He said he was happy in his adopted hometown, surrounded by family, friends, and other Somali expatriates. We talked about how Minneapolis and St. Paul became home to such a large Somali population, the largest in the country I later learned, having taken in some 25,000 emigrants since the early 1990s. And while Amiin never mentioned the decades-long civil war in his home country as his reason for relocating, I assumed that it played a part.

We also talked shopping malls. "This place has everything you need, it's a good mall," Amiin assured me as I signed my receipt, the taxi still idling at the curb. There was a hint of concern in his voice. He seemed, in some small way, to be overcompensating for something he said when I first stepped into his taxi. As we left downtown Minneapolis and headed southwest for Edina, Amiin had asked if I was certain that Southdale is where I wanted to go. He told me that most out-of-towners preferred to visit the Mall of America in nearby Bloomington, and noted that it would be no trouble to change course.

Amiin's recommendation wasn't lost on me. Mall of America is an architectural behemoth, part consumerist shrine and part sideshow spectacle—a one-size-fits-all experience that hosts an estimated 100,000 visitors per day and sprouts from the open expanse of Middle America like a small civilization. With 530 stores spread across three levels that span nearly 4.9 million square feet, it's the largest shopping mall in the country, a distinction held since it first opened in 1992. More baffling than its sheer size, however, is the scope of what it offers beyond shopping—an amusement park, aquarium, and children's museum to movie theaters, a comedy club, and flight simulators. But I wasn't in search of the daunting spectacle that the Mall of America promised. My intentions were more humble. I wanted to visit the wellspring of the American shopping mall, the historic and geographic location where this ubiquitous cultural entity first took root. When I told Amiin what made Southdale significant, and why I wanted to see it for myself, the explanation piqued his interest.

Opened in October 1956, Southdale Center is the oldest fully enclosed shopping mall in the country. With a sprawling architectural footprint covering 800,000 square feet, Southdale was almost immediately adopted as the blueprint for the regional shopping center of the future. While other cities boasted similar concepts at that time, most notably Valley Fair Shopping Center in Appleton, Wisconsin, which opened more than a year before Southdale, it was overshadowed by the sheer magnitude of its counterpart in Minnesota. Valley Fair, often referred to as the first "weather-protected shopping center" in the country, featured only six stores on a single level when it first opened. By contrast, Southdale's three levels, seventy-two specialty shops, two anchor department stores, and forty-five acres of parking gave the impression of a small city brimming with life.

Designed by Los Angeles–based architect Victor Gruen, a Viennese émigré and socialist, and developed by the Dayton Company, Southdale was imaginative from its inception. Gruen's vision for the mall, inspired by European-style piazzas and Greek agoras, was radical for its time. By 1952, when he was first commissioned to helm the design of Southdale, he had already established himself as an innovative thinker in the field of retail architecture, first through his writings and theoretical sketches, and later with the design of Northland Center outside of Detroit, which became an early example of mixed-use, retail development—featuring auditoriums, a bank, post office, infirmary, fountains, and lavish landscaping to complement the storefronts. And while Gruen's personal tastes were often reflected in his earlier architectural designs, his home city of Vienna greatly informed what his shopping mall in Edina would become. "Victor Gruen designed Southdale from memories of Europe," *Architectural Forum* rhapsodized in 1956.[1]

Not only was Southdale more lavish in size and scope than Gruen's previous projects, it was more ambitious in what Gruen hoped it could achieve conceptually. He wanted to bring European sensibilities stateside by dramatically blurring the lines between shopping, socialization, leisure, and play. What Gruen ended up introducing was an all-new, holistic consumer experience. And in no place were his ambitions better demonstrated than in the design of Southdale's civic spaces, particularly its center court.

This central square, named the "Garden Court of Perpetual Spring," was the crown jewel of Southdale Center. An oasis designed to captivate shoppers, it was a climate-controlled town square retrofitted for a new era. The court featured fountains, goldfish ponds, plants and flowers, an aviary, and commissioned works of art, including sculptures by Harry Bertoia. Beneath the skylights and amid the flora was an enticing eatery dubbed The Sidewalk Café, staffed by uniformed waiters serving tea and croissants to an equally well-dressed clientele. Pinwheel umbrellas colored red and white, and shoppers streaming in to find a place to eat and rest, gave the court an appearance of a city street bustling with activity.

In the evening, as nightfall dimmed the space, a soothing ambience was created by the glowing storefronts that opened on the garden court—their display windows brimming with merchandise arranged just so. As shoppers walked the concourses that fed into the court, they would window-shop or stop to rest, sitting at the edge of a fountain or pausing on a bench—the persistent sound of water at least acting as a reminder of tranquility if not a means to achieve it. Nearby brightly colored birds fluttered and sang in the court's two-story decorative cage, illuminated by a cluster of pendant lights, while the aroma of fresh-brewed coffee filled the air.

While most shoppers flocked to the garden court attraction, not everyone was impressed. During a visit to Southdale in November of 1956, Frank Lloyd Wright had little praise for what Gruen had built. "You've got a garden court that has all the evils of the village street and none of its charm," he said. "Who wants to sit in that desolate-looking spot?"[2]

Wright was mostly alone in his condemnation of Southdale. *Fortune*, *Newsweek*, and the *New York Times* all praised the new mall and its amenities. *Life* hailed Southdale as "The Splashiest Shopping Center in the U.S.," while *Time* christened it a "pleasure-dome with parking." Consensus, at least at that time, was most certainly in Gruen's favor.

Southdale was unique because it took the idea of an open-air shopping center and turned it inside out. Gruen's concept, with its fortress-like facade, still achieved a strangely alluring appearance thanks to the gleaming entranceways of Donaldson's and Dayton's, Southdale's two original anchor department stores. The mall teased shoppers with the promise of a rich and enticing interior world, an immersive experience entirely foreign to American consumers at that time.

Herman Guttman, who worked alongside Gruen and supervised Southdale's construction, realized at the mall's grand opening—which attracted 75,000 people—that there was something special about what they had built. "People came in and looked and their mouths opened," Guttman said. "The impact was phenomenal. There was nothing like it."[3]

As Amiin pulled away from the curb at Southdale, I walked into Macy's through a set of double doors, crossing a threshold identical to the department stores that anchor the dozens of malls in and around my hometown of Pittsburgh, Pennsylvania. Once inside the scent of perfume and new clothing hit me first, followed by the familiar aroma of French fries and pizza drifting from the food court. Reentry to the mall triggers a kaleidoscopic rush of memories—from your first visits as a child or the countless times you rode the Easter train at center court, to that afternoon as a teenager spent suit shopping for your high school dance or as an adult pleading with the clerk at customer service to issue a refund. Entering the mall is like tuning into an unbroken neural frequency, a signal at once individually unique yet universally relatable.

As I passed clothing racks, jewelry displays, and make-up counters, familiar landmarks seen and remembered from other malls, it was like following a map rendered in memory. I had never been to Southdale before, but I knew where to go. That's the promise of a mall's floor plan: the geography of repetition. If I were in a Macy's in Providence or Cincinnati or Reno or Bakersfield, the serpentine aisles would have led to similar concourses while only the names of the malls would have changed—from Warwick to Northgate, Meadowood to Valley Plaza. There would have still been skylights and white noise, Cinnabon and Muzak, security guards and information kiosks. The mall experience is predictable that way, like looking at a photocopy of a photocopy of a photocopy.

My trip to Southdale, in many ways, was a pilgrimage. While I am not religious, nor do I want to spiritualize my experiences, public spaces have long had a profound influence on me—from playgrounds and community parks to bridges, vacant buildings, and abandoned houses. My innate fascination stems from not only the escapism I looked for in these places as a young child or teenager, and later as an adult, but also in the shared personal histories they hold—offering an almost-tangible communion with past, present, and future.

As a boy, for example, I remember being drawn to the vacant house two doors down from where my family lived in the town of Wilkinsburg, Pennsylvania. I was 8 or 9 years old. At first I only peered through the windows, marveling at how normal it all looked inside—so much so that I almost expected to see a family appear in the dining room, or notice someone descending the staircase from the second floor. On my last visit, a friend and I managed to open a small side window in the living room above the mantelpiece and

I crawled inside. I sat atop the bookcase, my legs dangling as I surveyed the room. It was summer and the house was hot from being closed up, the air inside thick with dust. To be in a forbidden place sent adrenaline surging through my body, made my arms tremble. I couldn't bring myself to climb down the empty bookcase and investigate the rest of the house. I was too spooked.

By the time I was a teenager that fear had vanished. Public spaces offered a temporary distraction from the growing turmoil in my personal life, a string of years marked by a struggle with severe clinical depression, obsessive-compulsive disorder, and a destructive relationship with a girl that I loved. One of the places I often visited was the underside of a suspension bridge that gapped a valley in Pittsburgh's eastern suburbs, beneath a busy highway that fed cars to the nearby mall. I walked the girders with arms out at my side for balance, ignoring the three-story drop that would have killed me had one of my feet slipped. Whenever my tightrope walk grew old I explored the catwalks that crisscrossed the length of the bridge and mimicked the inbound and outbound traffic above. While my friends painted graffiti on the bridge's concrete support walls, the ground at their feet littered with spent Krylon cans and the discarded anti-theft cases of cassettes stolen from the mall, I often kept to myself. The quiet on those catwalks was hypnotic, accompanied by the rhythmic sound of car tires rolling against asphalt, a weird sort of adolescent lullaby that set me at ease as I looked out on the hazy wooded valley below, where train tracks sprouted from the nearby Union Railroad roundhouse and resembled a root system cast in iron.

The shopping mall, however, more than any other space, electrified my imagination. As a child, I viewed the mall as a sacred place of curiosity and wonder, its tropical gardens, waterfalls, and ponds the perfect backdrop for the make-believe worlds that I conjured. I associated it with the happiness of weekends, and time spent with my parents and older sister. As a teenager the mall is where I first experienced independence. I treated it as a small city to be exploited for everything it offered—rifling through albums at National Record Mart, Oasis, and Tapeworld, or shoplifting magazines and comic books from B. Dalton. With friends I ran wild through the hidden passageways behind the stores and evaded mall security when we pushed things too far; swooned over cute girls and even had my first kiss at the video arcade; abused free-refill policies and ate too many cheap tacos in the food court.

In adulthood, though, my relationship with the mall has changed. I've watched its prominence ebb and flow, witnessed how dozens have closed over the last decade while countless others flirt with obsolescence. I've come to see it as a once-sublime architectural marvel that struggles to make good on its initial promise of marrying community and commerce, a vision that Gruen established—alongside contemporaries like James Rouse and A. Alfred Taubman—and that legions of architects and developers have replicated for more than six decades. The shopping mall has also, in many ways, become a faded monument to the aspirations of post–Second World War Americans, whose embrace of the suburban dream was obsessive yet earnest, hard-won but fleeting.

While the shopping mall has been a constant in my life, it's also a place I've lost touch with. In Edina I hoped I might rekindle that connection. Not only because I wanted to better understand my personal history and psychological attachment, but because I wanted to investigate the mall's paradisiacal origins and how far it had strayed.

Sixty years after it first opened, Southdale had changed. My expectations for it were unrealistically utopic, as if I'd be walking into photographer Guy Gillette's picturesque images from the December 10, 1956, issue of *Life* magazine. But I had hoped that at least some of the mall's midcentury wonder might still be intact. Gillette's photographs told a story of the future realized in the present.[4] With Southdale, Gruen had successfully channeled the forward-looking optimism of America's space age but in practical application. Instead of applying his ingenuity to architectural renderings of spaceports or moon colonies, he tethered it to the terrestrial in hopes of mitigating the social isolation of the suburbs.

Southdale was more than a shopping mall. It was also a bold experiment in suburban planning. Gruen initially envisioned Southdale as the centerpiece of a much larger, mixed-use suburban development intended to encompass more than 800 acres. In his original plans, the mall was conceived as a social and retail hub that would anchor a thriving community comprised of apartment buildings, houses, schools, a medical center, park, and even a lake. Mindful that shopping malls were similar in theory to the downtown shopping districts they emulated, yet different enough to feel foreign and new, Gruen stressed the importance of communal spaces, open-air cafés, and play areas for children in an effort to provide "crystallization points for suburbia's community life."

"The basic need of the suburban shopper is for a conveniently accessible, amply stocked shopping area with plentiful and free parking," Gruen wrote in 1960. "This is the purely practical need for which the shopping center was originally conceived and which many centers most adequately fulfill. Good planning, however, will create additional attractions for shoppers by meeting other needs which are inherent in the psychological climate peculiar to suburbia. By affording opportunities for social life and recreation in a protected pedestrian environment, by incorporating civic and educational facilities, shopping centers can fill an existing void."[5]

Walking the Southdale promenade toward the garden court, it became clear that Gruen's attempt to fill an existing void in suburbia had inadvertently created others. Nowhere was this more evident than in the mall's once-vibrant central square. Aside from Harry Bertoia's *Golden Trees* sculptures, which still towered at center court, the space was cavernous and sparse. The only thing perpetual about the former Garden Court of Perpetual Spring was its sense of utter vacancy. All signs of

Gruen's communal oasis had been eradicated. No café or fountains or fishponds, no birds singing songs amid the din of conversation. No greenery. The garden had been removed from the garden court, replaced with Caribou Coffee and Sunglass Hut kiosks manned by underpaid employees, and occasionally serving as an intersection for mall guards sputtering by on Segways. It looked as if the lush and inviting scenes that Guy Gillette photographed back in 1956 had never existed, like it was all a mirage.

Southdale also had other voids beyond the faded grandeur of its garden court; none more glaring, perhaps, than the marginalization of small businesses, once integral to Southdale and nearly every shopping mall built from the mid-1950s through the late 1970s. That was before chain stores dominated the retail landscape, of course, when regional and independent business owners were among a shopping mall's primary tenants.

As I wandered from Southdale's well-appointed concourses, where retailers like H&M, Victoria's Secret, Banana Republic, Coach, and J. Crew were spotlighted, I discovered a different side of the mall. In less-trafficked side hallways, businesses like Dragon City Acupressure, Yan Boutique, Ala Moana Nails, and Stitch It Clothing Alterations were relegated to obscurity—placed at a noticeable remove from the mall's marquee retailers. This practice is not unique to Southdale. Malls across America often lease subprime space at discounted rates, which can be attractive for small businesses hoping to benefit from a mall's built-in foot traffic. But as I walked past these businesses set amid darkened, vacant storefronts, and in some cases adjacent to areas wreathed in construction sheeting, it was hard to view such lost hallways as anything but retail ghettos.

When Southdale was built in 1956, it entered a cultural environment far different than what exists today. Men were still the breadwinners and heads of the household, while women raised children and kept family life running smoothly. Shopping trips were a matter of necessity, not leisure. Since then, like nearly every mall in every city across the country, Southdale has weathered myriad social and economic changes. Southdale is now a Simon Mall, part of a nationwide conglomerate of malls with centralized ownership and branding. In other words, Southdale, once the archetype for the modern American shopping mall—acclaimed for its thoughtful design, lavish storefronts, and town-like atmosphere—has become just another banal franchise of the industry it inspired. While it may not be nameless, it has become faceless.

Late in life Gruen realized that his vision for the shopping mall had become increasingly unrecognizable. Not only were his designs altered in ways that baffled him, so too were his aspirations for what the mall could be. In place of experiential design, architects and developers obsessed over retail footprints, lease rates, and the maximization of selling space. As subsequent iterations of Southdale sprung up town after town, he came to view his creation as a "gigantic shopping machine" with few redeeming qualities. In Gruen's estimation, his concept had failed. Even though malls have become a makeshift social hub in the American suburbs, this less-than-perfect realization of the concept strayed too far from the Viennese architect's original vision.

"He revisited one of his old shopping centers, and saw all the sprawling development around it, and pronounced himself in 'severe emotional shock,'" Malcolm Gladwell wrote in 2004. "Malls, he said, had been disfigured by 'the ugliness and discomfort of the land-wasting seas of parking' around them. Developers were interested only in profit. 'I refuse to pay alimony for those bastard developments,' he said in a speech in London, in 1978."[6]

Gruen's vocal opposition to what malls had become offered a fairly damning commentary on their place in American society. It's also worth noting, at least for the sake of synchronicity, that the Viennese architect publicly disowned his creation the same year that filmmaker George A. Romero released *Dawn of the Dead*, a film in which four survivors seek refuge in a shopping mall overrun by zombies. The late 1970s signaled a turning point in not only the evolution of the mall but consumer culture as a whole. Shopping had evolved from leisure activity to national obsession. And while slogans like "Shop till you drop" and "Born to shop" didn't start appearing on T-shirts and bumper stickers until the 1980s, they would quickly become the dominant mindset. Against the backdrop of a highly consumerist culture, Gruen realized that his shopping mall concept had failed to spur the thriving suburban core he envisioned—and that its long-term sustainability might not have been feasible.

After walking the concourses at Southdale, it became clear that Gruen's successors had not improved upon his vision; they had merely bent it to their will. Since Southdale first opened, developers and retailers across the country have transitioned the shopping mall into a joyless but effective delivery system for merchandise—muting the importance of socialization and environment in the process, reducing the experience to nothing more than a transaction.

I traveled to Southdale in search of history, but the history of the mall wasn't there anymore. It's now omnipresent, distributed and replicated in every big city and small town across the country, and even around the world, not always with favorable results. Gruen's architectural dream—the perfect synthesis of people, place, and things—has been simplified to a capitalist recipe. And rarely has that recipe been repeated or improved upon, especially with the same care and attention that Gruen brought to Southdale. While his designs were by no means flawless, Gruen approached his work with a humanistic bent and the aspiration to build a place that was at once practical and magical.

Aspiration is key to a shopping mall—not only to its success, but also in its appeal. It is a hopeful place that perpetually embraces the new, where now is forever. And malls are aspirational not just for the architects who design them and the developers who wish to profit from their success, but also for the shoppers who seek comfort in their glimmering hallways. As Gruen wrote in 1964, the shopping mall was merely the latest iteration of an extravagant concept

British urban planner Ebenezer Howard had proposed as early as 1898: "As one of the features of the new garden city he planned a ring-shaped 'Crystal Palace' to serve as a 'shopping center' (he uses this very term). He writes, 'Here manufactured goods are exposed for sale, and here most of that class of shopping which requires the joy of deliberation and selection is done.'"[7]

Such joy is intrinsic to the appeal of a shopping mall. It's what attracts us there in the first place, and what entices us to return. Not only in the joy of deliberating over objects we desire, but in the joy of participating in the fantasy of the mall—suspending all disbelief and disappearing into a world within a world. When we visit a mall we seek an emotional experience. When we enter a dressing room and look in the mirror, we might see a better version of ourselves or perhaps the person we wish to become. In the furniture gallery of a department store we envision living rooms and dens and bedrooms more magnificent than what's waiting for us at home. Browsing housewares we imagine dinner parties with good food and interesting conversation. In record shops we search for music that will someday score our memories, coaxing a smile or prompting tears each time a favorite song is heard. Visiting a mall is as much about the future as it is about the past, as much about experiences that have happened as it is about experiences to come.

At Southdale, I felt no connection to its storied past. I couldn't envision Frank Lloyd Wright in his three-piece suit and pork pie hat opining to reporters about the mall's uninspired architecture. Nor could I picture the garden court alive with activity, shoppers engaged in conversation at the café, plant life illuminated in the background as sunshine poured through the skylights. And I couldn't picture the crowds that flooded the concourses on opening day in October of 1956, eager to experience everything that the mall had to offer. Maybe that was because I didn't grow up visiting Southdale. I had no emotional tether to the mall—no memories, no experiences, no personal history. As a child I had never tossed a penny in the fountain at center court and made a wish. As a teenager I had never shoplifted cassette tapes or lost hours playing Street Fighter in the video arcade. And as an adult I had never brought my sons to the mall as an escape from the winter cold and as a makeshift place to run free. By the time I visited Southdale all I found was the shell of what Gruen had built. While I wasn't surprised by that discovery, it still left me disillusioned.

As I retraced my path back to Macy's, I called Amiin and arranged for him to pick me up. It was almost closing time at Southdale and there were fewer people in the concourses, with foot traffic reduced to a trickle. Before entering the department store, I paused at a seating area in the end court. There was a couch, coffee table, chairs, and a cell-phone charging station, the type you normally find in an airport terminal. The scene reminded me of the domestic vignettes at IKEA, but without the mood lighting and staged clutter of possessions—books, framed photographs, vinyl LPs, and knick-knacks. An older woman sat alone on the couch, face illuminated by the screen of her phone, power cord draped across her lap. She didn't notice me, and for a few seconds we inhabited that odd and lonely space together, awkwardly.

In Macy's I followed the same serpentine aisles that brought me into the mall, but in reverse. I passed the same make-up counters and jewelry displays, noticed the same scent of perfume and new clothing, the aroma of French fries and pizza faint but still drifting from the food court. But this time none of it unlocked a torrent of memories. Maybe that was because I had already acclimated to the mall and the euphoric rush had run its course, dissipating more and more with each step that I took. Or maybe that was how all trips to a shopping mall ended, mind wrung out and ready to disengage.

When I stepped outside of Southdale Center night had fallen. The rain had slowed and so too had the flow of shoppers from the mall. Half the parking lot was empty, with cars at the far rows most likely belonging to employees sequestered until all security gates came down and the lights went dark. From around the bend a pair of headlights appeared and Amiin's taxi slowed to a stop at the curb.

"How was the mall?" he asked, turning the volume down on the radio as I slid the side door of the taxi open. He was smiling, his eyebrows hanging like a question mark.

"It was good," I said, unconvincingly. "Though I didn't buy anything." I was empty handed. No shopping bags, so I had little to report on that front. And something about my visit was nagging at me.

"I'm not sure I found what I was looking for," I added, pulling the door closed behind me before fumbling with my seatbelt. I realized how odd that sounded—particularly to a stranger I had met only a few hours earlier. But after seeing Southdale reduced to such an unremarkable place, devoid of the magnetism it once possessed, I couldn't help turning the idea over and over again in my head.

"That's too bad," Amiin said. "Maybe next time you visit Mall of America."

"Maybe," I said. "Next time."

PART ONE

CHILDHOOD

1 ETERNAL SPRING

On spring nights, when my mother worked the closing shift at Gimbels, my sister would roller skate up and down the sidewalk out front of the department store eagerly awaiting her return to us. As she floated back and forth in her white patent leather skates with the red wheels and red-and-blue laces, my sister looked lost in a deep, blissful peace—a nine-year-old girl at play on a makeshift roller rink lit by hundreds of towering light posts spread across acres of parking that radiated in every direction. Behind her the entrance to Gimbels glowed bright against a hazy blue-black sky. The sales floor was empty but still illuminated, a thousand fluorescent tube lights humming in unison as the last of the cashiers tallied their receipts for the night and emptied their registers.

I watched from the passenger seat of my father's gold Plymouth Duster, baseball game tuned in on the radio. It was 1981 and I was four years old. The Pirates were two seasons removed from winning the World Series, when the song "We Are Family" by Sister Sledge somehow became the team anthem and was played ad nauseam on every transistor radio and car stereo throughout the city of Pittsburgh. My father, whose interest in sports was casual at best, still preferred the radio to total silence. So the banter of play-by-play announcer and color commentator filled the space between us, populating the car with chatter other than our own.

Each time I heard the wheels of my sister's skates roll over the seams in the concrete—*bump-bump, bump-bump, bump-bump*—my eyelids grew heavier. Maybe because it was late and I was tired, or because the sound reminded me of falling asleep during long family road trips, only to wake as my father slowed the car off the interstate and passed over rumble strips cut deep in the road near every toll plaza.

"What's taking so long?" my sister yelled in a high-pitched voice, skating toward the car. "Shouldn't mom be done by now?" Her pixie cut bounced from side to side as she rolled, one skate in front of the other. I relayed the message to my father, who hadn't heard the request. Zoned out on baseball talk, he was ready to doze off when I tugged at his sleeve. He looked over at me, then back at the silver Seiko on his wrist.

"Your mother should be out soon," my father said, letting out a sigh before sinking back again in his seat. "Not too long now," I yelled, offering a big smile in my sister's direction.

What made Gimbels so appealing, besides that they employed my mother—and when we dropped her off at the start of each shift my father would often let me roam the colorful aisles in the toy department—was the fact that it was more than an average department store. It wasn't situated on a thoroughfare somewhere downtown, flanked on all sides by city streets thick with automobile and foot traffic, or sequestered in the odd purgatory of a strip mall dotted with shoe repair shops, pizza parlors, and supermarkets. Gimbels was different. It was an anchor store, a grand portal to the voluminous inner world of Monroeville Mall, a sprawling indoor shopping mall located in the suburbs east of Pittsburgh. It was a destination our family flocked to even before my mother worked there, a place that commanded our attention due to its grandeur and the allure of its contents. And while it was a place that loomed large in our lives, it was rare that we ever referred to it by its full or proper name. To us it was, and would forever be, the mall. No more, no less.

When it first opened in May 1969, Monroeville Mall embodied the quintessential shopping experience of the day. As one of the first indoor shopping malls in Pennsylvania, and at that time the largest in the country, it featured 125 shops anchored by three major department store chains—all housed in a climate-controlled environment intended to attract visitors year round. Like so many other shopping malls across the country—Southdale Center in Edina, Minnesota; Midland Mall in Warwick, Rhode Island; and Dixie Square Mall in Harvey, Illinois—Monroeville Mall was designed to act as both civic gathering place and consumer paradise. It was envisioned, like its predecessors, as a town center to feed and nurture the suburban idyll.

Embellished with tropical gardens, fountains, lava rock waterfalls, footbridges, and goldfish ponds situated between its myriad shops, the interior environment of Monroeville Mall encouraged visitors to suspend all disbelief and forget the world outside its doors. In summer it was a utopic, air-conditioned escape from the heat and humidity of Western Pennsylvania. During the winter months it offered warm refuge from the region's biting cold and its endless canopy of swollen gray skies and misty rain. It was, by design, a pleasure dome immune to seasonal change—a place that welcomed strangers from near and far to come inside.

At one end of the mall, a theatrical stage encircled by sunken seating framed the entrance to the Joseph Horne Company, while the Clock of Nations—a two-story clock tower featuring animatronic puppets that emerged on the hour, each representing the different ethnicities of Pittsburgh—stood in a large common area outside of Gimbels at the other side. Restaurants and lounges like the Brown Derby and Di Pomodoro dotted the upper and lower levels of the mall; and an indoor ice-skating rink dubbed the Ice Palace urged visitors to extend their stay.

Our family was happy at the mall. Part wonderland and part bazaar, it was a place that had nothing we truly needed yet everything we wanted. There were comic books and magazines by the hundreds at B. Dalton and hooks filled with action figures at Toyco, brand-new cars from local dealerships parked beneath the skylights in the main corridor and display cases gleaming with jewelry at Horne's. It was easy to lose track of time at the mall, to forget what brought you there in the first place. And at some point it almost became our family's second home, one of the places we felt most comfortable in our lives.

On weekly strolls through the furniture galleries at J. C. Penney, my mother indulged her quest for the perfect living room—a pursuit that often required the entire family's participation. My sister and I happily obliged, flopping down on a sectional sofa before turning our vacant gazes toward a Proptronics television set, attempting to mimic the same catatonic expressions we had mastered sitting on the couch at home; or pretending to argue over who staked a claim to one of the many astronaut or equestrian-themed bedroom sets intended to woo both parent and child. We were happy in our make-believe lives.

My father, however, had a more restrained approach. Meandering through the staged scenes of home life, he'd inspect a price tag or wrap his knuckles against a coffee table—a sort of impromptu quality check, he explained—while my sister and I rifled through dresser drawers searching for God knows what. Or I would notice him reading a detailed treatise from Scotchgard outlining the different ways their product might protect against a litany of accidents, namely the destructive behavior of children—whose tendency to vomit without notice, bleed at inopportune times, or spill large volumes of Kool-Aid were common hazards foreshadowed in the company's literature. Eventually my father would find comfort in a plush La-Z-Boy, pulling back on the wooden lever to eject the footrest as his whole body reclined in comfort. It was easy to picture him back home, sipping tea from his favorite mug as re-runs of *Barney Miller* flickered on our family's console television set. Meanwhile, seated at the edge of a nearby loveseat, my mother flipped through fabric swatches imagining which color or pattern might best suit our life.

Our trips to the mall were aspirational, fantasy play that allowed us to envision what our lives might look like if we had more money, or how our lives might flourish given different circumstances and accessories. Would a bunk bed with a hidden study nook make me a better student? Would an L-shaped couch with remote-control cozies and matching ottomans help us grow closer as a family? None of these questions were ever posed or even answered. Still, we indulged in real-time daydreams that projected a series of potential futures, each version outfitted with a different couch, kitchen table, or bedroom set. At the mall, we were only limited by how lavish a scenario we could conjure from imagination. Outside the mall, however, our lives were altogether different.

Our Duster parked at the curb outside the employee entrance, I kept my eyes trained on the brown metal door where my mother emerged each time we picked her up. It was a ritual we observed week after week, month after month, spring and summer, fall and winter. During the holidays when shoppers flooded to the mall, our pick-up service increased. My mother, who worked at the service desk handling merchandise returns and customer complaints, was also tasked with giftwrapping shopper's purchases. I imagined her job was glamorous, getting to dress up and punch keys on a cash register while alternately preparing gifts destined for display beneath some stranger's Christmas tree. To do work that sent happy customers on their way, arms loaded with gifts wrapped in silver-and-red paper and topped with sparkling bows, would be both magical and gratifying I assumed. It also seemed demanding, with an ebb and flow that took my mother away from us for long periods of time most nights and weekends. But we learned it was a finite disruption. In the cold quiet of winter, when all the money was spent and the hours of part-time employees cut, our visits became less frequent. Yet the waiting always seemed endless, like my mother might never materialize at that door. Like the mall might never give her back.

My sister and I were suspicious any time my mother strayed too far. Back home in Wilkinsburg, where we lived in a duplex with my grandparents, we could easily keep tabs on her whereabouts. Still my mother had places where she would steal away. If the telephone cord was stretched thin and trailed out the kitchen door onto the side porch, we knew she was on a long distance call with my aunt from St. Louis and wasn't to be bothered. Or when we heard the faucet on the porcelain tub turn on with a squeak, it signaled that my mother was drawing a bath, which meant I could sit outside the door and fire off question after question until I got bored. If my mother arrived in the living room wearing a pair of earrings, or holding car keys in her hand, we either demanded to know where she was going or implored that she take us along. And the times we couldn't find her, my sister and I would sit at the bottom of the steps to the second floor and listen for her voice, convinced she had snuck away to sit and talk with our grandfather while he smoked Pall Malls and listened to chatter on his police scanner. Since so much of our time was spent with my mother, it felt unnatural to be apart.

Each time the door to the Gimbels employee entrance popped open, more people filed out. Some I recognized, others I didn't. There were the sullen men dressed in blue suits and black suits, gray suits and brown suits—salesmen of all ages and varieties. As they lumbered through the empty parking lot, deep coughs erupted from their chests as plumes of blue cigarette smoke gathered overhead. I knew their type, if not their faces. These men sold stereos and televisions, mattresses and bed frames, stoves and refrigerators. They smelled of Old Spice, coffee, and tobacco; had heads of varying shapes and sizes topped with white, wispy hair or dark, mop-like patches; wore yellowed mustaches on their faces or propped heavy-framed bifocals on the bridges of their nose; carried breath mints in their pockets and believed their own persuasive talk.

As more employees streamed out the door, I searched for my mother in the crowd. She would be out any minute now. As the salesmen drove away in their Buicks and Fords, pretty saleswomen in white blouses and tan skirts walked side by side beneath the bright parking lot lights. They chitchatted and laughed and smiled like they were at a party, having more fun than you could possibly imagine. Some carried purses while others had the handles of brown shopping bags draped across their delicate forearms. I imagined these women were smart and had good taste in music, that they went dancing at the nearby Holiday House when they weren't on the clock, and that their boyfriends and husbands worked as lumberjacks or baseball players or bus drivers—each job equally exotic from my vantage point as a child.

A certain sense of mystery surrounded each employee that exited the mall, from the weary expressions on their faces to the body language that telegraphed joy or boredom or defeat. I didn't know these people, but I wanted to. Like the young, blonde-haired women who worked at the cosmetics counter administering beauty advice, or spritzing perfume samples on small paper swatches intended to entice customers to open their wallets. Or the clusters of wild-eyed twenty-something men who worked in the warehouse driving forklifts or balancing refrigerators on dollies. These men, often dressed in dirty white T-shirts and jeans, reminded me of background characters you might see in an episode of *Starsky & Hutch*: dock worker, truck driver, hoodlum, patsy, informant.

Something about the way these men and women carried themselves piqued my curiosity, especially as I watched them shake off the weight of the workday on their march across the parking lot. They seemed to come alive or at least normalize to the reality around them. It was fascinating to watch the transition, like actors unwinding backstage after a performance. But it also offered a candid look at the divide between employees and customers. If you worked at the mall, it didn't necessarily mean you shopped there.

When shopping malls first appeared in America in the mid-1950s, department stores like Gimbels were central to the appeal of these new and attractive retail environments. Adorned with the names of their wealthy founders, stores like Bloomingdale's, Belk, Macy's, Saks Fifth Avenue, and Kaufmann's aspired to offer sophisticated experiences to affluent customers. And though malls and their shops were never intended as exclusionary spaces, their pricing and suburban locations required a certain level of access—namely, middle-class salaries and a car. While shoppers with deep bank accounts may have arrived in search of fur coats or designer housewares, your average visitor came for the otherworldly experience that the mall offered.

As the stream of employees thinned to a trickle, it was harder and harder to stay awake. Faced with a similar situation, Bugs Bunny would have employed toothpicks to keep his eyelids from snapping shut. But I was never convinced that would actually work. The world outside the car had also become increasingly quiet. Each time I dozed off, my head would fall forward and I would startle awake.

"Mom's coming," my sister squealed, waving her arms wildly as she skated toward the car. My father, as if on cue, sat forward in his seat and turned the key in the ignition, bringing the Duster back to life. As the engine rumbled he turned the volume down on the Pirates game before looking over in my direction. "Okay, jump in the back," my father said, motioning with an outstretched thumb to the spot behind him where I normally sat. He leaned across the passenger seat and pulled the metal handle, pushing open the heavy door with his right arm. My sister rolled up in her skates, stopping herself by putting her hands on the hood. When my father folded the passenger seat forward so I could get in the back, I saw my mother walking toward me. She kneeled down on one knee and opened her arms, an invitation to run full tilt toward her. I took off across the sidewalk while my father was still convincing me to sit in the backseat. As the soles of my sneakers gripped the concrete, my mother's smile and her bright eyes and sandy brown hair grew closer and closer until we collided.

"I missed you so much," I told her, my arms slung around her neck. She smelled like perfume and air conditioning and the scent of newness that permeated every corner of the mall.

"Did you bring me anything?" I asked. She held me tight for a moment longer, extending the euphoria of our reunion, before reaching into her purse. I was eager to know what surprise she had chosen. When her hand emerged she held a small white bakery bag between her index finger and thumb, the name Daisy Donuts printed on one side.

"Thumb print cookies?" I asked.

"See for yourself," she said, handing me the bag with a smile. When I opened it there were two small cookies inside, each with a daub of chocolate icing in the center and yellow sprinkles dusted around the edges. I hugged her again, the white paper bag still clutched in my hand. As my sister skated over to give my mother a hug, I turned and saw that my father had stepped out of the car and was watching the scene unfold. When my mother finally stood up she took my hand and my sister's in hers as we walked back to the car. I could feel the cold imprint of her wedding band against my skin, and every so often she gave my hand a little love squeeze.

"Tell us everything," my sister pleaded, her eyes wide with anticipation. "We want to hear about crazy customers, all the gifts you wrapped, and the weird things people tried to bring back to the store."

2 PARADISE UNKNOWN

Our human landscape is our unwitting autobiography,
reflecting our tastes, our values, our aspirations, and
even our fears, in tangible, visible form.
                    —PEIRCE F. LEWIS, *THE INTERPRETATION OF*
                                        ORDINARY LANDSCAPES

The scene is picturesque in black and white, the horizon
crumbling, as if the photograph, dated 1966, had been taken
against a fading hand-painted backdrop. Facing the camera
a line of businessmen, ceremonial shovels in hand, stand
atop a snow-covered hill in Pittsburghs eastern suburbs.
Behind them in the distance a pair of transmission towers
loom on a wooded ridge, electrical wires strung like black
arteries above a stand of trees that stretch further east into
oblivion. Out of sight dozens of newly minted housing plans,
christened with names like Garden City and University Park,

dot the lush hills where cows once grazed, while down in the valley a bustling four-lane highway threads from the city to the toll plazas of the Pennsylvania Turnpike and beyond.

In the photograph, some of the men—dressed in three-piece suits and overcoats, fedoras and black-framed eyeglasses—smile and pose for the camera, shovels speared in the dirt. Others miss their cue, heads turned to the side, awkward expressions forever captured on their faces. Among those pictured include Eugene Lebowitz, his son Edward Lewis, and son-in-law Mark Mason, and Harry Soffer and his son Donald, all partners in a land development firm known at that time as Don-Mark Realty. The occasion for the portrait was celebratory: a groundbreaking at the future site of Monroeville Mall, a two-level enclosed shopping center that would be one of the largest in the country once completed. On that winter day, however, as the men stood side by side on that hilltop, fresh-turned dirt at their feet, their presence echoed a larger cultural shift that had been taking place since the late 1940s in cities all across the country.

Whether you lived in Cleveland, Chicago, Oakland, Detroit, or of course Pittsburgh, people, predominantly whites, were fleeing the uncertainty of the city for the promise of a second chance in the suburbs. No more crime, drugs, and declining property values. No more failing schools. No more neighbors whose complexion frightened you. No more fear of the future. To begin again was the plan, away from ghettos and the weed-like persistence of urban blight and the creeping menace of poverty. A fresh start for a generation fixated on the future and rocketing to the moon; a generation obsessed with forging a new reality, where old habits and old problems and old places were kept at a safe remove.

Nowhere in America were issues of urban renewal and suburbanization more visible or scrutinized than in Pittsburgh of the mid to late 1960s. Renaissance I, an ambitious slate of redevelopment projects that were started after the Second World War and lasted until the early 1970s, had begun to transform the city from a smoky industrial hub best known for steel production to a modernist metropolis poised for the future. This citywide upheaval, spearheaded by Richard King Mellon, Mayor David L. Lawrence, the Allegheny Conference on Economic Development, and the Urban Redevelopment Authority (URA), focused national attention on Pittsburgh, attracting the input, interest, and critiques of such luminaries as Robert Moses, Lewis Mumford, and Jane Jacobs. Documenting the city's historical transformation even became a decade-long project for Stefan Lorant, the renowned editor and photographer whose comprehensive tome, *Pittsburgh: The Story of An American City*, defined the latter half of his career and helped foreground Pittsburgh for a national audience.[1] But as redevelopment continued into the late 1960s, when the URA attempted to remake neighborhoods like East Liberty in an effort to stanch population loss, the forces of suburbanization were already underway.

"People wanted something new; they wanted either a new house or a new road or a new playground or a new school, and that was all available in the suburbs," said Robert Pease, former executive director of the URA. "It was also affordable; through FHA you could borrow money and buy a house. People moved to the suburbs for those things, but the lack of knowledge as to the implications of living there and working in the city, I don't think were foremost in anybody's thoughts."[2]

The exodus from Pittsburgh's inner city is how a once-rural town like Monroeville grew in population from 8,000 residents in 1950 to 33,000 by 1976.[3] Why farmland was parceled out into lots for middle-class families to buy and build on, how land developers became kings. The landscape was being dramatically transformed by a widespread case of postwar panic that, by 1970, had permeated mainstream consciousness enough that even singer B. J. Thomas, in a lulling ode to white flight, wondered why he was suddenly alone in the city: "Where have the people gone/Seems like there's no one hangin' on/Look through the window/The houses are empty/Hey, everybody's out of town/Seems like I'm the only one around."[4]

Of course Thomas wasn't alone. Legions of people were being left behind in the cities, namely minorities and low-income residents unable to afford the transition to the suburbs. In Pittsburgh, while urban renewal had bolstered the city's national profile, it had also displaced generations of families from their homes. The Lower Hill District, for example, once a rich multicultural community of African Americans—as well as Italian and Jewish immigrants—was razed to make way for the construction of the Civic Arena. That redevelopment pushed Italian and Jewish immigrants to relocate to neighborhoods like Bloomfield and Squirrel Hill, where they created strong ethnic communities that still exist today. But African American families were scattered far and wide, to city neighborhoods like East Liberty and Homewood—places where white families were increasingly selling their homes—and outer boroughs like Braddock and Rankin. America's postwar plans of a better tomorrow in the suburbs looked very much to be an aspiration limited by race and class.

Shopping malls of course played a role in emptying the cities, drawing customers and their money away from main-street and small-town businesses to the crystal palaces being built just beyond the city limits. By the early 1960s, Pittsburgh, like most cities across the country, had a contingent of shopping malls cropping up beyond its borders, with Northway Mall (1962) and South Hills Village (1965) in the suburbs north and south of the city, Allegheny Center Mall (1965) on Pittsburgh's North Side, and Greengate Mall (1965) in nearby Westmoreland County. And customers weren't the only ones leaving Main Street behind. Some shop owners intent on embracing change traded in their long-established storefronts for a lease in a mall, while others viewed declining sales as a sign of the times and shuttered their businesses for good. When considering the impact that shopping malls had on traditional retailers at the time, Dan Smith, a professor of marketing at the University of Pittsburgh, noted that the phenomenon was like "putting four magnets around the city and sucking people out."[5]

In many ways, it's impossible to tell the story of the shopping mall without at least acknowledging its significance to the development of the American suburbs. From the beginning the two have existed in a closed-circuit economy. If you lived in a housing plan, you shopped at the mall. If you shopped at the mall, you lived in a housing plan. Many housing developments predated the emergence of the shopping mall. But in many small suburban towns, shopping malls were a response to those developments. In Monroeville, families fleeing to the suburbs had made their homes in places like Turnpike Gardens and Garden City—which boasted the types of houses in the types of neighborhoods that promised the idyllic suburban life that so many Americans longed for in the wake of the Second World War.

"In April 1955, Wanda Jennings, Mrs. America of 1954, was on hand to greet visitors at the opening of the latest development in fully planned community living—Garden City in Monroeville, Pa.," boasted a brochure for the new housing plan. "This 600-acre development would be built partly on farmland owned by the Graham family near the center of Monroeville. Designed and constructed by the Sampson-Miller Associated Companies, it would offer 1,500 three and four-bedroom homes at moderate prices."[6]

A year before ground was broken for Monroeville Mall the same developers opened South Hills Village, one of the city's first fully enclosed shopping malls and the largest, at that time, between New York and Chicago. After a ribbon-cutting ceremony where John K. Tabor, Pennsylvania's state secretary of commerce, lauded the creation of 1,000 new jobs, a "Christmas-size throng of shoppers" was unleashed into the mall. Not only was South Hills Village an indicator of Pittsburgh's willingness to embrace the future of retail development, Tabor stressed that it was a key example of how the city's "healthy and growing industrial foundation" had paved the way for such a venture.[7] In other words, steel production and manufacturing might are what brought the shopping mall to Pittsburgh, offering legions of blue-collar workers a gleaming new place to spend paychecks earned while toiling in the mills.

The success of South Hills Village set the stage for the developer's new shopping center, Monroeville Mall, which would be even more ambitious in both size and scope. It's why many of the men in that photograph from 1966 are smiling. The promise of the mall had already shined on them, and they had a good sense of just how lucrative the future might be. But a groundbreaking marks more than a new beginning; it also signifies the end of what came before.

In Monroeville, agriculture came first. Like so many other rural towns eventually swallowed whole by suburbanization in the 1950s and 1960s, the land had long been its most precious commodity. Known as Patton Township until the early 1950s, farms first dotted the hills and valleys when it was a rural enclave, but it soon became widely identified as coal country—and companies arrived en masse to extract as much as they could from its rich seams. With the construction of the Penn-Lincoln Parkway and Pennsylvania Turnpike, Monroeville was also rapidly becoming a gateway to the east. Motels, lounges, nightclubs, restaurants, car dealerships, and discount stores sprung up almost overnight along the surrounding highways—making the once-sleepy town a place where all the spoils of suburban life were readily available. Expansion was so rapid and lucrative that even the mafia was impressed. Michael Genovese, head of the Pittsburgh family, built the Phoenix Motel and the Toll Gate Motel to serve as money laundering operations.[8]

When developers proposed building a shopping mall on a 280-acre tract of land once home to a strip mine owned by the Thomas Harper Coal Company, residents in Pittsburgh's eastern suburbs were skeptical. Would people stray from Route 22, a heavily trafficked nearby highway, to visit a shopping center hidden high atop a hill? How would this new mall be any different from Miracle Mile Shopping Center located less than two miles down the road, or nearby Eastland Mall in the Electric Valley?

There was also little frame of reference for such a sprawling retail facility. Shopping malls were still a relatively new concept gaining momentum across the country. It had been only a decade since the opening of Southdale Center in Edina, Minnesota, the nation's first enclosed shopping mall. Since then, malls began opening in dozens of cities and small towns across the country. There was Westfield Garden State Plaza (1957) in Paramus, New Jersey; Maryvale Shopping

City (1959) in Phoenix, Arizona; and Del Amo Fashion Center (1961) in Torrance, California.

These sprawling shopping centers showcased and facilitated a new lifestyle, one that aligned with the country's excessive and increasingly suburban mindset—and they created a strange facsimile of urban shopping districts but in a setting so vast it was almost unrecognizable from its predecessors. As writer William Severini Kowinski once described it, the shopping mall was like "Main Street in a space ship."[9]

With everything consolidated under a single roof—retail, services, dining, and leisure—the conveniences of the mall were intoxicating. So much so that early advertisements for Monroeville Mall bragged that it was "Built for Lazy Shoppers," with customers able to get "from any point in the mall to any other point in less than five minutes."[10]

It was as if suburbanization and the emergence of the shopping mall had ushered in a new system of beliefs, where laziness was now a virtue and convenience trumped personal initiative. It was a distinct departure from the postwar optimism that permeated 1950s America. In the same way the do-it-yourself movement—a billion-dollar industry by 1954—had encouraged young homeowners to buy power tools and build their own future, the shopping mall almost begged consumers to shirk their responsibilities, venture indoors to a climate-controlled Shangri-La, and just be. In a short amount of time, consumers evolved from active participants to passive loiterers. It was a stark contrast that dovetailed with the ever-growing ambitions of Madison Avenue's silver-tongued ad men and their onslaught of sales pitches—many of which increasingly viewed consumers as sponges ready and willing to do nothing but soak up clever catchphrases and jingles.

In the edition of the *Pittsburgh Press* published the day before the mall's grand opening, which featured a Monroeville Mall advertising supplement that rivaled the size of a small newspaper, marketers heightened the emotion of their prose.

"All hands point to Grand Opening Day tomorrow . . . when Monroeville Mall opens its doors for the very first time!" The advertisement boasted of the mall's 125 stores and "enormous selection of high quality shopping," with the phrase "Only hours away" invoked as a trance-like refrain. The ad, which featured a graphical silhouette of the Clock of Nations—the mall's 32-foot, $125,000 clock tower built by Los Angeles–based designer Gere Kavanaugh—also noted the uniqueness of the mall's architectural features. "Only hours away . . . an extraordinary clock tower, rising from the interior of the mall, set to entertain hourly with animated lifesize puppets . . . plus a new rink-le in shopping . . . an indoor ice-skating rink, larger than Rockefeller Center's, for year 'round skating.'"[11] And perhaps most relevant to Monroeville Mall's appeal as an all-weather, retail oasis was its sales pitch as a "virtual all-electric city under one roof, with regulated temperatures 12 months a year."

Earthly delights notwithstanding, the mall also aspired to nourish shoppers' spiritual needs. "The mall is the center of community life and the church must be there," said Reverend William M. Paul, founder of Monroeville Mall Ministry. "It's a contemporary example of how the church may serve people's needs—by going to where they are." As the *Post-Gazette*'s John Little wrote at the time, "The [ministry's] aim will be to assist people, some 250,000 shopping there weekly, in problems from men's clothes to men's souls."[12] Every last detail, it seemed, had been considered.

When Monroeville Mall opened on May 13, 1969, thousands of people arrived to revel in the much-anticipated spectacle, an event advertised on television and in newspapers for weeks in advance, with its developers announcing that "Big Time Shopping" had finally arrived in Pittsburgh's eastern suburbs.[13]

"It's here . . . beautiful brand new Monroeville Mall . . . bringing you the best of the Big Time department stores . . . all set to dazzle and delight . . . to intrigue and excite every single shopper. Here's a shopping complex with its very own personality . . . dramatic, sophisticated, stimulating . . ."[14]

On that morning in May, local celebrities, politicians, and retail executives gathered at center ice in the mall's skating rink for a ribbon-cutting ceremony. Don Riggs of WQED Television, perhaps best known as the voice of Willie the Duck on the local children's program *Safari*, served as master of ceremonies for the event. An ice-skating demonstration kicked off the festivities and introduced an assortment of guest speakers—including the men of Don-Mark Realty, the mall's developers. Of the men who were pictured holding ceremonial shovels in that black-and-white photograph from 1966, all were in attendance that day: Edward J. Lewis, Don Soffer, Mark E. Mason, Harry Soffer, and Eugene Lebowitz. They stood alongside County Commissioner Leonard C. Staisey; Richard R. Pivirotto, president of the Joseph Horne Co.; Herbert A. Leeds, president of Gimbels; and John J. Duncan, mayor of Monroeville.

When the guests of honor finished with their remarks, the Gateway High School Marching Band started to play. As mayors and developers and executives exited the Ice Palace, and as eager shoppers flooded the mall's gleaming concourses and common areas, the marching band's music trailed behind them. Trumpets and trombones and clarinets echoed throughout the mall. Snare drums and bass drums rattled and boomed off the shining terrazzo. The promenades, illuminated by sunshine breaking through the skylights, were filled with the white noise and overheard conversations of curious people. Among the lush tropical plants, water fountains, and elegant storefronts, visitors stood transfixed by all that this new shopping mall had to offer.

3 SPACES BETWEEN

My mother was finishing a phone call in the kitchen when she shooed me to the patio. Her head tilted to the side, receiver cradled between shoulder and ear, she searched in vain for the keys to her Firebird parked out front. We had errands to run, she told me, and would be leaving soon for the mall. As I stepped out onto the side porch, the screen door clacking against its wooden frame, I hurtled down a short flight of steps before running alongside our red brick house toward the front yard.

It was late afternoon and the summer air smelled sweet, a mixture of honeysuckle and fresh-cut grass. It was 1986 and I was nine years old. Dressed in a T-shirt, shorts, and sneakers, I sprinted back and forth across our patio, a patchwork of stone pavers that my father and grandfather laid several years before. I had cut that same invisible path a thousand times. With the fresh air filling my lungs, I passed beneath the pine tree where the birdhouse with saloon doors hung year round, the spring hatchlings already grown up and gone for the year. Making the bend past our cinderblock front porch I disappeared in the shadows between our house and our neighbor's, making a U-turn in the narrow strip of dirt where I still sometimes played with Matchbox cars, even though I worried I was getting too old for toys. From the gap between the houses I barreled back toward the patio, my hand bouncing on top of the waist-high wire fence that bordered our steeply terraced front yard, which was like running along the edge of a two-story cliff.

"We're leaving soon," I heard my mother yell from inside the house to my sister, who had been sitting on the blue floral print couch in the living room, reading a book. As I ran I thought about all the things I would do when we got to the mall. How I would throw pennies in the goldfish pond or follow the stepping-stone path that vanished within the tropical gardens or beg my mother to let me play video games at the arcade.

Out of breath I stopped to look out on the neighborhood. Our house sat atop a hill at the intersection of Franklin Avenue and Princeton Boulevard in Wilkinsburg. I liked to pretend it was a watchtower—the place where I could survey all the people who came and went in the neighborhood, keep an eye on the cars that passed through on their way to someplace else. Wherever those strangers were headed I assumed it was more important or more exotic than what our block had to offer. Boredom often felt cruel in that way, convincing me that something better was always happening just out of sight. But I had remedies for boredom, ways to augment reality.

If I shook my head fast from left to right I could see all of Princeton Park in a dizzying blur—from the row house apartments my parents called the Rabbit Hutches, where newborn babies appeared every nine months, to the Green Hill at the opposite end of the street; from the Vacant House two doors up and Kenny Denny's white van two more past that, to Brenda and Derrick's death-drop staircase and the crumbling sidewalk that disappeared around the bend. It was homemade euphoria to see everything at once while standing still, the neighborhood compressed into a color wheel of bricks and grass and fences and cars.

If I wanted to summon supernatural powers I'd bury my eyes deep in their sockets, squeeze my eyelids tight until jagged white bolts of lightning struck against the black oblivion inside my head, and as I opened my eyes I'd see an electrical storm crackle up Franklin Avenue and spider web across the boulevard where my parents parked their cars. Except that afternoon the space where my father kept his pale green Camaro, which he bought from a co-worker for only $100, was empty. Oil spots on the asphalt marked its absence as I counted the hours until he returned from work. I was eager to play catch with my father, feel the weight of the baseball landing in my Denny McLain hand-me-down mitt.

"Time to go," my mother said, pulling the front door closed behind her as she motioned for me to follow. For a second I imagined the mall and the toy department at G. C. Murphy and was overcome by a rush of joy. My sister close behind, we started down the steep and crooked staircase, which was bordered by a railing fashioned from plumbing pipe on the left-hand side, and led down to the street below.

The steps were made of poured concrete that crumbled more with each passing year. Everyone in our family had had a near-death experience on those steps, mine being the time my sister accidentally launched me from the edge of the staircase while I was still seated in my fire engine pedal car. Luckily a next-door neighbor intervened, grabbing the backend of the pedal car as the front wheels took flight. If not I might have split open my skull or broken my arm or ended up in a crumpled pile on the sidewalk below, which would have spelled trouble for my sister.

"Shotgun!" my sister called at the bottom of the steps, staking her claim as my mother's co-pilot. She was always more organized than me when it came to social situations, particularly an outing to the mall. It was often too late by the time I remembered, though I didn't mind riding in the backseat. A trip in my mother's Firebird was reward enough, like strapping into a starship. It didn't matter where I sat. As my sister folded the passenger seat forward I jumped in the back, sinking deep into the black leather upholstery as she slammed the heavy door shut behind us.

"You okay, kiddo?" my mother asked as she took her seat behind the steering wheel, the unturned key chiming in the ignition. Her eyes met mine in the rearview mirror and she flashed a quick smile. It was the type of gesture that always made my heart feel full. As she heaved the driver-side door shut, she started the engine, which roared to life in an instant.

My parents found the Firebird in the Pennysaver. I remember the night we drove out to the country to pick it up. I was still dressed in my Catholic school uniform, khaki pants, and an Oxford shirt, which was wrinkled from a long day sitting in class. We drove until we reached what felt like the middle of nowhere, an open landscape of winding roads and endless guardrails, until we finally arrived. When I saw the Firebird I fell in love. Its Kelly green paint was tinted with silver and gold flecks that shimmered in the fading daylight. The rear end of the Firebird was lifted like a muscle car, and the big back tires reminded me of racing slicks—the same kind I'd seen on Don Garlits' dragster when my father and I watched the NHRA races each weekend on TV. I couldn't believe this was our new car. It looked like a Hot Wheels, one I would have played with until the wheels were loose and the paint wore thin. I imagined we would own it forever and that my mother would eventually hand it down to my sister who would later hand it down to me. That night in the country, however, as my mother sat behind the steering wheel for the first time—gushing with excitement—you could see her imagining all the places we'd go.

On the drive down Franklin Avenue to the stoplight at Johnston Elementary School, the car rumbled as if the engine block had come loose under the hood. It was a mix of power and fragility, which meant we might rocket down the road when the light turned green or sputter onto the boulevard and stall. It was impossible to predict; the Firebird was temperamental in that way. When the light turned we roared onto Ardmore Boulevard without pause. Windows rolled down and the warm summer air rushing in, we passed the auto body shop and produce market on our left, headed for the intersection near the Texaco station and Ford dealership. That's where the on-ramp to the Parkway East was located, our high-speed portal to Monroeville Mall.

As the light turned yellow and traffic stacked up, we cruised slowly past the house where my sister's friend Gina lived. During the school year, on rare occasions when my parents both worked early and couldn't drive us to St. James, Gina's mother looked after us in the morning. It was always a welcome break from our normal routine. We would eat Eggo waffles smothered in Jif peanut butter and watch cartoons until it was time to leave. I always talked to Gina's older brother Joe. He went to high school at Central Catholic in Oakland and liked to breakdance. He also had a Run–DMC poster in his room, and told jokes that I laughed at but didn't always understand. When it was time to go, we would all pile into their family's station wagon and head for school.

At the red light, my mother pushed in the cigarette lighter on the Firebird's dashboard and waited for it to get hot. Leaning over toward the floor at my sister's feet, she pulled a Viceroy from her purse. Waiting for the lighter to pop out felt like listening for the microwave to ding. The glowing coils always enamored me. I wondered how hot it would be to the touch, what kind of mark it might leave on my skin. When the lighter popped back out my mother pressed the orange-red coils against the end of her cigarette and took a puff. Seconds later blue smoke twirled from her nostrils as she slotted the lighter back in place.

"Look," my mother said, "it's our friend." She was pointing to a mountain of a man with long gray hair running the full-serve pump at the Texaco. My mother and father often used the phrase "our friend" when mentioning one of the many recurring characters in our lives—whether it was the stern crossing guard near Johnston School, the panhandler by the Turnpike who looked like a disheveled university professor, or our eccentric substitute teacher Ms. Buttonhole. To imagine these people as a loosely connected cast of supporting characters was fun. It's how we interpreted the world around us to make it our own. Each time we passed our friend at the Texaco we noticed his pants falling down, offering anyone within eyeshot a glimpse of his pale and hairy backside. Over the years he had earned a reputation at that intersection, eliciting car horns and colorful responses from motorists and passersby each time he unintentionally mooned them.

When the light turned green my mother stepped on the gas pedal and the Firebird lurched forward with a burst of speed. Aimed at the on-ramp to the Parkway we gained momentum as we passed beneath the green highway sign that read "Monroeville," with the road ahead of us curving sharply to the left. As we hit the overpass and crossed above the inbound traffic, we entered a stretch of the road that was like a tunnel with no top, where two tree-dotted hills rose up on either side of the car. For a few short moments it felt like we were driving through the woods in a remote part of the world—no clutter of houses on the hillsides, no gas stations or fast-food restaurants spoiling the view. I often fantasized about living on top of those hills, nestled among the trees in a clubhouse built from scavenged wood. *Could you live there without being bothered?* I wondered. *Would anyone ever know?*

As the hills on either side of the Firebird receded, the road ahead straightened out. I could see the busy highway from the driver-side window. Cars, trucks, and motorcycles rushed past in an endless stream. From a distance it all looked fake, the traffic reminding me of slot cars on a plastic track. Some were headed southwest toward downtown, others eastbound for the Turnpike and destinations in Harrisburg, Philadelphia, and beyond. I thought about the mall as I looked out the window, picturing the space where my mother would park the Firebird in the lot outside of Gimbels. It had been several years since she worked there; still, entering the mall through the glass doors of that department store had become a ritual. Other than the classrooms at St. James and the quiet of our house in Wilkinsburg, the mall was familiar in a way that always made me feel safe.

As we prepared to merge, I pretended that we were in deep space surrounded by stars and nebula, part of a caravan of intergalactic travelers destined for exotic worlds. In my mind, our Firebird was the Millennium Falcon and the on-ramp was hyperspace. When we merged I pictured my mother pushing the gearshift forward to engage the hyperdrive as we disappeared in a blink, leaving the starfield behind us slowly turning clockwise as an unseen orchestra swelled in our absence.

4 SHOPPING IS A FEELING

In November of 1977, filmmaker George A. Romero arrived with cast and crew at Monroeville Mall. The young director, who by that time had established himself as a pioneer in the horror genre, was set to start production on his latest film, *Dawn of the Dead*, a sequel to his 1968 cult classic *Night of the Living Dead*. Once again Romero's slow-shuffling ghouls—starved as always for brains and entrails, meaty thigh bones and plump jugulars—would be unleashed on bumbling humans ill-prepared for a world gone rotten.

This time around, however, Romero, who in *Night of the Living Dead* touched on issues of race in the civil rights era, had plans to skewer a new social dilemma: the rise of the American consumer. And to properly lampoon the nation's burgeoning shop-till-you-drop culture, Romero needed the ideal backdrop.

"Right then it was just really the beginning of that mall culture where you went there and you hung out all day," Romero said in a 1997 interview with the BBC. "My impression of walking through there, going through this sort of ritualistic, unnatural, consuming experience, was that we really do become zombies in here. And the way the music was lulling . . . everything about it was just so hypnotic. It seemed like nothing was real in there."[1] The hypnotic experience that Romero observed when he first visited Monroeville Mall is one that's now ingrained in the American psyche.

For those who frequent shopping malls the oddly euphoric rush experienced upon entry is often triggered by a mixture of familiar sights, sounds, and smells. Among architects and urban planners, this sensation is sometimes referred to as the Gruen Transfer or Gruen Effect, named after Victor Gruen, forefather of the American shopping mall. It is defined as the moment when shoppers are "so dazzled by a store's surroundings that they will be drawn—unconsciously, continually—to shop."[2] It also relies on a certain amount of confusion, the idea that once consumers enter a shopping mall they lose track of their original intentions, becoming more susceptible to make impulse purchases. Elaborating on this idea, cultural historian Norman M. Klein has explained how a shopping mall's labyrinthine design, much like that of a casino, can also elicit feelings of "happy imprisonment," in which consumers have "infinite choice, but seemingly no way out."[3]

Happiness is intrinsic to how we experience a shopping mall. Aside from personal desire, and how it prompts us to wish we owned certain objects, happiness is what urges us to return to the mall time and again. Not only to experience it in a new place for the first time, but to recapture it and relive it and allow it to color our memories. It was no fluke that when Romero first visited Monroeville Mall to scout it as a location for *Dawn of the Dead*, he noticed its hypnotic effect on people. Nostalgia and a sense of longing are baked in to the DNA of all shopping malls, an emotional failsafe designed by their creator.

"Gruen's projects . . . all reflect the same philosophy and share the same features: a nostalgia for a community you can trust, architectural forms that recall the past and people-centered European streets," wrote Giandomenico Amendola. "The Gruen strategy builds on people's longing for a world in which they feel safe. The underlying model is the traditional community and the everyday life of small provincial cities or of European historical towns, enriched by elements of Disneyland's Main Street. Nostalgia, filtered by historical and mass media stereotypes, has proved to be a powerful and effective strategy."[4]

Generations have come to know the shopping mall through personal, often highly emotionalized transactions— from small children who play in the wide-open atriums to teenage boys fawning over girls in the food court; from adults who seek refuge from the summer heat to retirees in search of early morning exercise. And though the American shopping mall never became the vibrant town center that Gruen envisioned—a suburban hub of retail, medical, residential, and recreational facilities—the institution itself has come to transcend the mere act of shopping.

"Our experiences take the built environment of a mall and add meaning to it," said Ross Schendel, a retail historian and co founder of the website Labelscar.com. "They create memories because people are socializing and having these experiences together. When malls replaced downtowns in the mid-20th century, they became the de facto gathering place for those living in suburbs, and created these collective experiences and fond memories we have."

Nowhere is that collective emotional experience more thoroughly examined, and lampooned, than in the David Byrne film *True Stories* (1986), set in the fictional town of Virgil, Texas. Byrne, who plays the role of unnamed stranger in the film, narrates his visit to the local mall as if hosting a current events program on public access—complete with deadpan delivery.

"The shopping mall has replaced the town square as the center of many American cities," Byrne explains. "Shopping itself has become the activity that brings people together."

Wearing a black Stetson and a yellow western-style button-down shirt, Byrne surveys the people of Virgil as they stroll the well-lit thoroughfare at their local mall. He passes a quintet of businesswomen dressed in identical suits who speak in unison ("Oh, hi. I just got off the plane."), and a stern-faced grandfather lecturing his grandchildren as he escorts them from the mall.

"In here, the music's always playing" Byrne says. "What time is it? No time to look back."

His delivery is straight-faced, often breaking the fourth wall to directly address the viewer. Byrne's trip through the mall acts as a sort of anthropological survey, offering a stylized portrait of the shopping mall in the mid-1980s, healthy doses of absurdity peppered throughout. As he approaches a bookstore, for example, a chorus of laughter gives him pause.

"Starving peasants sell their bodies to vampires for blood money," says a man choking back laughter as he reads the headline of a tabloid. Overweight and dressed in khaki pants and a striped Polo shirt, the man is a living portrait of American excess and the rampant hubris of the Reagan years. His friend, wearing almost identical clothing, is doubled over with laughter, leaning against the magazine rack for support. Byrne playfully smiles while shaking his head and walking away.

"The stores here are pretty clean," he continues. "The air's fresh, there's plenty of parking, plenty of space to walk around."

When he spots a man rushing from an electronics store, arms loaded with purchases, they strike up a friendly conversation.

"Hi, how are you?" Byrne says to the man. "How come you're not at work?"

"Oh, I'm working on a project at home," the man tells him.

"I send signals up," he adds, his eyes looking up.

"Oh, to satellites and things like that?" Byrne asks.

"Well, further than that I hope," the man says, shrugging his shoulders. "Hey, listen, I gotta get to work before all hell breaks loose."

In the fictional town of Virgil, Texas, like real towns all across the country, the shopping mall was as much a destination as it was an emotional support system. It was a place to congregate and unwind and spend money. But it also signified that shopping was more than a utilitarian pursuit—it was a feeling to be attained.

"People here are inventing their own system of beliefs," Byrne says, eyes staring out at the audience. "They're creating it, doing it, selling it, making it up as they go along."[5]

PART TWO

ADOLESCENCE

ADOLESCENCE

5 LITTLE BOXES

In the summer of 1988, when I was eleven years old, my family traded our duplex in the city for a Cape Cod in the suburbs. We moved six miles east of Monroeville Mall to a housing plan called Regency Park, which was the exact same distance from the mall as our old house. It was almost as if our family was anchored—physically and spiritually—to the mall as ground zero in our lives.

After years wasted on wishing some stranger would buy our aging duplex in Wilkinsburg, my parents ended up signing it over to the real estate agency, a decision that relegated our former home to a tragic future as rental property. I didn't want to leave the place where I was born. The house where I took my first steps; where I first learned to ride my thrift-store bicycle on the crumbling sidewalk that disappeared around the bend; where my sister and I tore open presents each Christmas morning as my parents watched, tired but happy. To leave my friends behind was even worse. But it was inevitable. The neighborhood was falling apart around us. All of our friends and neighbors were leaving or had already left. Drugs had moved in. Gunshots grew louder and closer each year. Vacant houses were turning up like weeds. No buyers or sellers wanted to live in a neighborhood past its prime, let alone fork over any cash to do so. That truth threatened the possibility that we would ever get out of Princeton Park, and it left my parents crestfallen. They took the deal and never looked back.

We moved to a town called Plum, where the schools were better and the houses were newer and everyone was white. Hidden among a tangle of two-lane roads and farmland, it was a landscape dramatically different from the city. The houses weren't squeezed together as tightly, and the neighborhoods lacked the physical boundaries of blocks. Instead the homes unraveled in an infinite loop, half a dozen midcentury designs stamped out in recurring patterns and built on the ground where farmers once worked, an unbroken white line painted several feet from the curb wrapped like a ribbon around it all. While my parents had only moved our family twelve miles east, it turned out to be a world apart. Privately I wondered if we had made a terrible mistake.

In Regency Park the white boys were different than the black boys I'd grown up around. They wore faded concert T-shirts with images of horned demons and laughing skulls. Rode dirt bikes and threw rocks at neighborhood cats. Shot BB guns at birds or empty soup cans strung up on clotheslines. Set things on fire so they could watch them burn. Some smoked cigarettes. Others chewed tobacco, collecting the brown spittle in the empty Mountain Dew bottles or cardboard pints of Turner's Iced Tea they'd discard alongside the roads. Near the Turnpike overpass that sliced through the neighborhood, the weeds were infested with litter—Twinkies wrappers, spent Budweiser cans, and grease-dotted McDonald's bags scattered like thistles in an overgrown yard—partial evidence of the teenagers I had seen roaming the housing plan in small herds.

More evidence was written on the walls, particularly in a cryptic message from the future: _Stoners Rule '89_. Those words were everywhere that summer. They were written in black spray paint on the Turnpike overpass and scrawled on the giant rocks in the quarry behind the low-rent apartments on Boulder Drive; carved into the red paint on the stop sign near the dental offices on Miller's Lane and scribbled in black Sharpie on the garbage can outside of Bill's Pharmacy.

I didn't know what a stoner was but I had some ideas. It was a term I associated with a group of longhaired older boys from the neighborhood who wore Rush T-shirts, jeans, and high-top sneakers. They looked more like men. I assumed that a stoner drank beer and smoked cigarettes and experimented with drugs of some kind, but I wasn't entirely clear on the details. The same way, in grade school, I didn't always know what the graffiti in the boy's bathroom meant.

From the window of my father's blue Caprice I kept watch on our new neighbors. It's how I knew the Ferry boys tore down the transmission for their Chevy Nova most weekends, and how I found out Mrs. Charlton, a mom who didn't look anything like a mom, sometimes laid out topless on summer days. First time I saw the Savilles string up a dead deer on the side of their house and cut open its belly with a hunting knife was from behind the glass of the passenger-side window, talk radio tuned in on the dial as we rolled past. And when I watched the Pale Man mow his lawn each week like a machine set on a fixed grid, it was on Saturdays as we backed out of the garage, ready to run errands.

In those early weeks after the move it seemed we had a reason to go to the store almost every day. Our first night in the house my mother was convinced she needed a new set of curtains for the picture window in the living room. I think she felt exposed with our new home lit up for the whole neighborhood to see. It was like a fishbowl, but not the lived-in kind with green algae on the glass and a blackened light bulb in need of replacement. We were the new fish trapped in a plastic bag floating atop the water—acclimating to our surroundings, figuring out how to live.

My mother wasn't alone in how she felt. The isolation of the suburbs washed over me like a slow-simmering fever in those first days. My response seemed part culture shock and part depression. Each afternoon I retreated to our backyard and climbed the towering maple tree, pressing play on my Walkman once I was at the top. Obsessed with Huey Lewis and the News, I listened to *Sports* and *Fore!* until the tapes wore thin. But after a while the cheery disposition of those albums no longer matched how I felt. From my perch two stories up I surveyed the neighborhood, getting to know the faces and behaviors of the new people all around us.

We lived among teachers, mail carriers, and janitors, bus drivers, nurses, and real estate agents. Neighbors came and went in minivans and station wagons. When they returned their trunks were filled with store bags—sometimes from the grocery store or nearby pharmacy, often from the mall. Of the places that I knew and where I felt safe, the mall, for better or worse, remained a constant. It was around before the move and remained significant after.

- didn't like neibarhood
- unComfortable
- Mall helped
- New kids are weird

6 WHITE DENIM

Teens at the mall are almost preternaturally skilled in the semiotics of fashion.

—BRUCE DOBLER

°goth lifestyle

From the moment I found my white denim jacket on the clearance rack at TJ Maxx it remained standard issue. No drastic alterations, no brash statements. I didn't cut off the sleeves, making a biker-style vest, or sew on a back patch pledging allegiance to a single band like Megadeth, Anthrax, or Motörhead. I understood that type of dedication was reserved for stoners and metalheads older and wiser than me; guys who had part-time jobs and wallets and mustaches, smoked cigarettes and drove cars held together with junkyard parts and body putty. They certainly didn't accompany their mother to Pier 1 Imports on a Friday night while she shopped for candles, or occasionally wet the bed after drinking too much root beer late at night.

As far as I could tell, these were the type of boys who spent their Friday nights revving car engines in the parking lot at the mall before disappearing to a housing plan to drink liquor stolen from their parents' kitchen cabinets and have sex with girls. And not just any girls, but the kind who emptied a can of Aqua Net on their hair, wore sleeveless Motley Crüe T-shirts, and skintight acid-washed jeans with black lace threaded up the side of the leg. These girls fascinated and baffled me, pumped blood below my waist and made me lightheaded. They also scared me. Where did they come from? Did they have parents or were they wards of the state, lorded over by a wrathful headmistress and penned up each night in some sleazy dormitory where they fought over cigarettes and phone privileges like characters in a USA Up All Night movie. As an eleven-year-old boy, girls and sex were still a mystery I hadn't figured out.

The year after I moved to Regency Park, my friend Mark and I found a rain-soaked magazine lying on the ground beneath the Turnpike overpass, near a tangle of garbage in the weeds. Some of its pages had come loose and were spread across the road. When I stepped closer I saw photographs of naked women. One picture of a woman sitting on a chair with her legs wide open was near the yellow dividing line. Another, which showed a dark-haired woman cupping her breasts in her hands while arching her back and looking with closed eyes toward the sky, was on the far side near a storm drain. It was the first time I ever saw pornography, unless of course you count actress Juliette Cummins' motel room striptease in *Psycho III*. As Greyhound buses and speeding cars rushed past above us, Mark and I stared down at the exposed pages. An advertisement featuring a "Strap-On Jack"—a large black rubber penis that fastened around the waist like a belt—was all that remained of the back pages.

The first time that I wore my white denim jacket was at Greengate Mall, a destination mall my parents went to when they got bored of the mall closest to our house. It was a 45-minute drive east on the Pennsylvania Turnpike, and we usually made the pilgrimage in fall or spring—my mother liked to time our trip with the change of seasons. In fall, the trees along the Turnpike turned brilliant colors as the leaves died, from burnt orange to deep burgundy and all shades of red. And in spring you could catch the forest coming to life again, skeletal tree limbs wreathed in green buds as distant dogwoods blossomed pink and white amid the towering hemlocks and pines. To venture through the mountains and valleys was as much a part of the experience as walking the concourses at Greengate.

Deciding to wear my white denim jacket felt uncomfortably bold. Maybe because I was too aware of its crisp sleeves, the denim so coarse it was like wearing a jacket made from light-grit sandpaper. Or because the word IRREGULAR was stamped in red ink on the leather tag inside the collar. After it had languished in my closet for weeks, I took the jacket from its hanger and pulled it on, partially obscuring the Magic Johnson T-shirt I was wearing, which featured a caricature of the Laker great spinning a basketball on his finger. It was one of several similar T-shirts in my wardrobe: Michael Jordan, James Worthy, Larry Bird, and Spud Webb. I loved basketball, but was starting to worry that it clashed with my growing interest in rock music. How could I like the Chicago Bulls *and* Def Leppard? The contrast worried me because the two interests seemed incongruent.

Each time we visited Greengate Mall it reminded me of a no man's land. Located in a rural swath of Western Pennsylvania, it was an area I associated with dirt bikes and Confederate flags, hunting rifles and pick-up trucks with Yosemite Sam mud flaps. By the time I frequented the mall as a teenager in the early 1990s, its shine had started to fade—a sad fact given my personal connection. We had gone to Greengate Mall since I was a young child. My grandfather, my mother's father, loved everything about it—especially the pageantry of its seasonal displays. Namely, Christmas and Easter. In one of our old family albums, there's a photograph from the early 1980s where my sister and I are posed for a portrait in the Christmas display, white pom-poms and striped candy canes all around us. My sister is smiling, as always, but my face is beet-red, staring down at a giant lollipop that had just fallen on the ground.

During the day Greengate's center court glowed, sunshine breaking through the skylights to illuminate the lush vegetation and glistening water fountains, which cast ambient sound throughout the concourse. And at night center court came alive, like a bustling village lit by lanterns strung in celebration. Greengate felt very much like a place out of time, as if it existed in its own dimension. Shoppers still gathered for coffee at the lunch counter in G. C. Murphy's and birds fluttered in a decorative cage placed among small trees in the food court; senior citizens lapped the upper and lower levels while men and women paused for conversation at benches in the thoroughfare. Everything felt simpler at Greengate, less burdened than life back home.

Kids my age and teenagers roamed the halls. But because they were all strangers, I wasn't as self-conscious to be in public with my parents, a growing concern at the time. After moving to the suburbs, I discovered that most kids I went to school with weren't necessarily spending time with their parents. Instead they were going places together, like mini golf, roller rinks, school football games, and the mall. It was a change that seemed to happen overnight, when I wasn't paying attention.

In a mirrored hallway near the food court, on my way to the newsstand at Tobacco Village, I caught sight of my reflection. It was the first time I had seen myself in the white denim jacket. After slowing down in an attempt to inconspicuously check myself out, I decided that buying the jean jacket had been a smart choice. It was a rare moment of self-confidence—so much so that it remains sticky in memory. The jacket even seemed to work with my high-top Nike Flights and Levi's 501s, at least as far as my odd, Marty McFly aesthetic was concerned.

At Greengate I always stopped at Tobacco Village to pore over the latest issue of *Heavy Metal* magazine, where I searched its pages for artwork by Frank Frazetta, Boris Vallejo, and Simon Bisley. Escaping into dangerous realms where barbarians reigned and scantily clad warrior-princesses would slit your throat had become a pastime. Fantasy, like the mall, offered a temporary escape from the growing isolation I felt in the suburbs. Tobacco Village is also where I picked up basketball cards—first collecting Fleer cards, and later NBA Hoops and Skybox. Each time I brought my purchases to the cash register, I worried the clerk might shame me for my weird, seemingly schizophrenic selections. But a balding old man with a snuffed-out cigar plugged into his mouth was usually who waited on me, and he could care less.

My white denim jacket was the first clothing choice I made, or at least the first piece of clothing that signaled an attempt at personal style. In this case, it was an aesthetic that declared: *I am an eleven-year-old boy who has recently discovered rock 'n' roll*. I unabashedly decorated the bright white breast pockets of the jacket with pins and buttons from my favorite bands, the way a proud grandmother might decorate her refrigerator with drawings from her grandchildren. There was a Hard Rock Café pin shaped like a Gibson Les Paul guitar, a gift my mother picked up on a business trip; square buttons with cover art from David Lee Roth's *Eat 'Em and Smile*, Def Leppard's *Pyromania*, and Van Halen's *OU812*—each purchased from a spinning rack near the cash register at National Record Mart in the mall.

As I waited to meet my parents in the food court at Greengate, I sat at a table near Burger King leafing through my copy of *Heavy Metal*. All around me were teenagers I didn't know. Some were older, some younger. I noticed older guys wearing Guns N' Roses T-shirts and girls with bleach-blonde hair and bangs teased high. Sitting there in my white denim jacket I wondered if anyone had noticed me, or if that moment in the mirrored hallway was just a fluke—a lapse in judgment.

I imagined a scenario where an old rock 'n' roller took a shine to me. On his way through the food court he walked in my direction before stopping at my table. The old timer was grizzled and wearing a beat-up leather jacket, a black-and-white skull stitched on the back. He pointed at the empty chair across from me, as if to say, "Do you mind?"

"Be my guest," I said, trying to act the part, still leafing through my magazine as if unfazed. The man reminded me of Sam Elliott, or at least some version of him I had conjured in my mind. When he sat down he reached in his pocket and pulled out a box of Marlboro Reds.

"Care for a smoke?" he asked, flipping open the lid of his battered Zippo.

"No thanks," I said.

"Smart man," the old timer replied. He lit his cigarette and the ember glowed orange as he took a drag, blue smoke twirling from his nostrils like signals sent as a warning. It was quiet for a long time as the man took in everything swirling around us—the people, the white noise, and the hum of the mall. Finally, he leaned in toward me, ready to say something. I leaned closer so I could listen.

"Pay no mind to what none of these fools think," he said, the words deliberate and slow as he spoke. "They don't know you." He looked at my jacket, squinted his eyes to get a better bead on the buttons and pins, before a wide smile spread across his weathered face.

"Know what I like about you? You know the secret," the old timer said. He leaned over and tapped his index finger on the breast pocket of my jacket. "White denim don't fade."

7 MALL MADNESS

You are standing in a shopping mall. But this is not the mall you normally frequent, or even the mall you drive to when you get bored of the mall closest to your house. The surroundings are familiar yet oddly nondescript. None of the store names register in your memory, retailers like M. T. Wallet's, Frump's Fashion Boutique, Scratchy's Records, Dingaling Phones, Chip's Computers, Yuppy Puppies Pets, and Sweaty's Sports. Where have all your favorite stores gone? It's as if you've discovered an entirely new shopping mall in a different part of town.

Hundreds of shoppers roam the brightly colored concourses and promenades, passing in and out of their favorite shops. But the faces of the men, women, and children are obscured, impossible to discern no matter how close you get. And there is no noise in the mall, no overheard conversations or the distant squeals of laughter from a children's play area, or even the sound of Muzak in the background. There are no smells, either. No aroma of pizza or French fries drifting from the food court, or the strong scent of a department store perfume counter stocked with fragrances by Liz Claiborne, Colors by Benetton, or Camp Beverly Hills. It reminds you of the dreams where your senses are dulled or where you lose control of some part of your body—where you try to talk but can't open your mouth, or try to walk but have no control of your legs.

You are wearing your favorite pair of denim overalls and that cute pink turtleneck you got for Christmas. Your hair is frosted and teased and your pants are pegged, ankles lost in a fluffy coil of pink socks. Your Keds are fresh from the box, their white canvas pristine. Your best friends are there too, girls with names like Shannon, Brenda, and Courtney. They're dressed in the cutest outfits and each of the girls is smiling at you, as if to say "Now it's your turn."

When you look down you notice $200 and a shopping list in your hand. It contains six items, jotted down in no particular order and in handwriting that you don't recognize. It's unclear how you arrived at this conclusion, but you somehow know that this list is your key to success. Acquire the products before your friends and you can leave the mall. Fail to do so, however, and your future becomes unclear.

"Attention mall shoppers," a voice bellows from the public address system, breaking the silence. "Sale at the Shoe Store!"

"Oh my God!" Shannon, Brenda, and Courtney scream, in unison, before giggling and running off to buy shoes. As they leave you behind you notice that each girl's arms are loaded down with shopping bags, as if they've been here for hours. Aside from $200 and a shopping list, as well as an Easy

Money credit card that you find in the front pocket of your overalls, you haven't even started to shop.

"It's no use," you whisper to yourself. "I'll never be able to catch up with my friends." That's when you notice a nearby sign for Coneheads Ice Cream and decide to walk in that direction. When you reach the register, you place your cash on the counter before ordering a double scoop of cookie dough ice cream in a waffle cone. It's your favorite flavor, and always lifts your spirits when feeling sad. Mom bought it for you that afternoon you left cheerleading tryouts in tears. And dad always gets you a cone at that little corner ice cream shop when you stay at his apartment every other weekend. When you sit down on a bench at the edge of the food court, something catches your eye. You notice the name Milton Bradley engraved in the floor at your feet. *That's strange*, you think. *Why is that name so familiar?*

* * *

When Milton Bradley first released its Mall Madness board game in 1988, it did so at the zenith of the shopping mall's popularity. Not only was the mall a pop culture phenomenon at that moment, shopping had become the nation's de facto pastime. Phrases like "Born to Shop" and "Shop Till You Drop" transcended bumper-sticker slogans and T-shirt designs; they had become mantras for legions of mall devotees. It was no surprise then that a board game set in a fictional mall appealed to both teenagers and adults. Even with instructions that urged players to obey the electronic

"Voice of the Mall" at all times, a concept as Orwellian as it sounds, players never flinched. Resisting the will of the mall was not an option.

The premise of the game was simple: first player to purchase six items on their shopping list and reach the parking lot was crowned winner. And gameplay was tailored to allow mall experts—namely young girls, eleven to sixteen years old—the opportunity to test their skills as budding consumers. Armed with cardboard shopping lists, plastic credit cards, and paper money, players were set loose in a two-story mall and reminded to spend wisely. Not only did the game recreate, in miniature, the prototypical mall of the 1980s, it acted as Milton Bradley's less-than-subtle way to train future shoppers.

Mall madness, however, was more than a game. It also denoted a condition that a large swath of the population was experiencing: an impulse to shop, socialize, and, to a high degree, tune out the noise of the world. With the turmoil of the 1980s roaring outside its walls—the AIDS epidemic, the rise of crack cocaine, the false hope of trickle-down economics, and the Cold War's ever-present threat of nuclear annihilation—shopping malls became a safe space. Not only for adults who on weekends sought refuge from their jobs, but for adolescents forming their identities and searching for a place to belong. Teenagers flocked to the mall with every intention of making it their own.

Nationwide fascination with shopping malls and their appeal prompted countless examinations, both academic and journalistic; at the root was an overwhelming desire to quantify the behavior of a mall's most devoted user: American teenagers. One particular study, Kathryn H. Anthony's "The Shopping Mall: A Teenage Hangout," epitomized the many attempts to decode teenagers' attraction to the mall's open spaces and endless corridors. "Most adolescents . . . admit to being regulars at the mall, verifying the phenomenon described by many . . . popular writers," Anthony wrote. "Their regular presence does not seem to embarrass them. On the contrary, many seem to take pride in their use of the mall."[1]

In Anthony's observations, there's an insinuation that teenagers should almost feel a certain sense of shame about time spent at the mall. But her view overlooks the shifting cultural paradigm: unabashed enthusiasm for the mall. Not necessarily enthusiasm for shopping, but for inhabiting an environment both familiar and enticing—a place that transcended commerce and offered asylum to suburbia's driftless youth. However strange it might sound, to be a mallrat was to be part of something bigger. Not only part of a scene, but an established social system of ritual and reward.

By the late 1980s, retailers, corporations, advertisers, and media companies viewed malls as part captive audience and part focus group—resources to be mined. And malls became a delivery system for not only consumer goods, but prepackaged culture and entertainment as well. Pop singer and teen idol Tiffany exemplified that type of transaction. In 1987, after the release of her debut album and the failure of its first single, Tiffany's manager booked a nationwide tour of shopping malls for the singer. 'The Beautiful You: Celebrating The Good Life Shopping Mall Tour '87," which was sponsored by Toyota, Clairol, and Adidas, launched at Bergen Mall in Paramus, New Jersey, before traveling to ten malls across the country.

"We wanted to take her to where her peer group hangs out all summer long—shopping malls," her manager Brad Schmidt told the *Los Angeles Times*. "If 'Tif is going to make it, she's going to do it first among 12- to 18-year-olds, and what better place to expose her than in America's playgrounds, the malls."[2]

Tiffany's shopping mall tour represented a larger trend: the mall as a micro arena. Prior to peak mall hysteria, central courts had often played host to local talent shows and even the occasional traveling spectacle—from go-cart races to bear wrestling. But by the mid to late 1980s, mall promotions had become a cottage industry—with firms like Shopping Center Network, a Miami-based mall promotions company responsible for shows like "Pets Are Wonderful" and "Take a Kid Fishing," producing performances in malls across the country. By 1988, MTV had even tossed its hat in the ring, launching its Museum of UnNatural History, a six-month, 27-mall tour billed as "Epcot Center meets Barnum & Bailey for young adults."

Due to such sustained national fascination, the mall remained a staple in films as well, including *Night of the Comet* (1984), *Weird Science* (1985), *Commando* (1985),

True Stories (1986), and *Bill and Ted's Excellent Adventure* (1989), with Genghis Khan, Abraham Lincoln, Joan of Arc et al. inciting chaos in the concourses at San Dimas Mall. In *Smooth Talk* (1985), a lesser-known film based on a short story by Joyce Carol Oates, a young Laura Dern attempting to make sense of her sexuality stars opposite a menacing Treat Williams, whose character becomes increasingly possessive of her throughout. Of course not all films with the mall as a backdrop are as nuanced. Many, like *Invasion U.S.A.* (1985)— which stars a denim-clad Chuck Norris killing Communists with his signature Uzis and roundhouse kicks—use the mall as a symbolic prop representing American ideals, while others fully embrace its potential for fantasy and kitsch. In the horror film *Chopping Mall* (1987) malfunctioning security robots gruesomely dispatch teenage employees inside the fictional Park Plaza Mall after close. "Where shopping costs you an arm and a leg" is the film's tagline, which makes it easy to understand how it's become a cult classic.

Perhaps most iconic of all, *Fast Times at Ridgemont High* (1982) uses the mall as a setting steeped in teenage uncertainty and emotional vulnerability. When ticket scalper Mike Damone shares his five-point plan for talking to girls with Mark "Rat" Ratner, it sounds like a conversation you might have overheard at your own local mall. That authenticity, surfaced in dialogue written by Cameron Crowe, addresses the mystery of teenage girls and the nonsensical nature of the male ego and epitomizes the tenor and tone of mall culture at the time.

"First of all Rat, you never let on how much you like a girl," Damone says, sidling up to a cardboard stand-up of Debbie Harry outside a Ridgemont Mall record store. "'Oh, Debbie. Hi.'" Damone acts unfazed as he circles the Blondie singer; Rat looks on, making mental notes. "Two, you always call the shots. 'Kiss me. You won't regret it,'" Damone says, slyly putting his arm around her shoulder. "Now three, act like wherever you are, that's the place to be. 'Isn't this great?' Four, when ordering food, you find out what she wants, then order for the both of you. It's a classy move. 'Now, the lady will have the Linguini and white clam sauce, and a Coke with no ice.' And five, now this is the most important, Rat. When it comes down to making out, whenever possible, put on side one of *Led Zeppelin IV*."

Not all films focused solely on teenagers' dependency on the mall; some offered subtle commentary on the nation's shopping addiction from an altogether different vantage point. In *The Blues Brothers* (1980), the artifice of the mall is quite literally laid to waste as the pair drives recklessly through the interior of Dixie Square Mall in Illinois, police cruisers in close pursuit as shoppers flee and dozens of storefronts are demolished. "This place has got everything," Jake says to Elwood, sirens flashing in their rearview mirror.

While mall madness may have peaked by the late 1980s, it's worth noting that its origins date back to the days of the very first shopping malls. For example, when Greengate Mall first opened in Greensburg, Pennsylvania, in 1965, it was wildly popular, so much so that the public almost didn't know how to cope with what the mall had to offer. They seemed to be experiencing what author William Severini Kowinski referred to as "agoramania."

"They couldn't get enough of the marketplace," he wrote. "The mall courts were constantly jammed, the stores flooded with gawking and buying humanity. According to stories I heard from reliable sources (like my sisters, who both worked there, and my father, who was the first manager of the Singer store in Greengate), the sheer quantity and accessibility of products in such a concentrated space seemed to push some people over the edge. There was a man who grabbed an entire rack of suits from a Greengate store and tried to run out of the mall with it. Another man scooped up an armload of record albums at the National Record Mart and charged down the escalator with a security guard in hot pursuit; tellers in the Dollar Savings Bank saw albums flying in the air as the two men disappeared on their way to the first level."[3]

* * *

"You're hungry," The Voice of the Mall intones. "Meet a friend at the pizza shop." You look around. The food court is empty. You're the only person within earshot. It sounds as if the mall is beckoning to you. Standing up from your seat, you walk over to an illuminated directory of stores. The pizza shop is at the other end of the mall, next to Dingaling Phones. You decide to take a walk.

Window-shopping as you stroll the concourse, you notice a few cute tops you might like to buy. You feel better than before, and the lump in your throat has started to fade. Out of the corner of your eye, you notice a pair of hot pink sunglasses that you're dying to try on. As you walk toward Made in the Shade Sunglasses, you bump into Shannon, Brenda, and Courtney.

"Where have you been?" the girls ask in unison. "We thought you got lost." Last you saw them they were running off to the sale at the shoe store, leaving you behind. But maybe you were supposed to follow.

"You'll never guess who we just saw at the shoe store," Courtney says.

"Who?"

"Todd," she says. "And he was with Melissa."

"Oh my god," you say. "But he just broke up with Heather last week."

"I know," Shannon chimes in. "And I heard a rumor that Todd kissed Kim at Tony's party on Friday."

"What a creep," you say.

"Who's hungry for pizza?" Brenda asks, and you and your friends rush into the pizza shop and find a booth. You are all back together again and, for a moment, everything feels right.

8 NEON HALLWAYS

You are here

"Look here boys, the asshole vibrates!" said the dough-faced woman behind the counter at the adult newsstand, her plump index finger pointed at the battery-operated anus of an inflatable sheep. "It's guaranteed to get you off."

There was a wildness in the woman's eyes as she spoke from her pulpit several feet above the sales floor, behind a cash-register counter loaded with scented oils, Astroglide, and penis pens; a wall teeming with dildos and butt plugs the backdrop for her performance. From beneath a pile of permed hair, her tone was part carnival barker and part infomercial huckster, and something about the expression on her face left me feeling even dirtier than the fact that I was standing in a smut shop on the last night of the year.

"You boys like what you see?" the woman asked, taking a long drag from her Virginia Slims cigarette, the filter stamped with the bright red imprint of her lipstick. "If not, there's plenty more where that came from." Smoke streamed from her nostrils as she motioned with her arm toward the rest of the store, well aware that she was pulling the curtain back on a world of hardcore imagery and explicit gadgets certain to explode our hormone-drugged teenage minds.

It was New Year's Eve 1991. With the mall closed we had nowhere to go. If you plotted our psychic points of interest on a map, only a handful of landmarks bore mention. The mall would carry a star like a state capital or major city. It was the center of our small but isolated universe of tract homes, rolling hills, abandoned industrial sites, schools, and retailers—a landscape defined as much by its ever-encroaching sprawl as the ongoing subtraction of its natural beauty. While it was by no means a cultural hub, the mall was the best we had. In descending order of importance was the Taco Bell in Miracle Mile Shopping Center, where we ate most meals; Boyce Park basketball courts for playing pick-up games until exhaustion set in; the New Jack Bridge, a blank slate for graffiti; and of course Ralph's Army Surplus. Not only did Ralph's fulfill our need as teenage boys to hold souvenir grenades and browse military-grade cutlery, it also nurtured our nascent fashion sense—introducing us to flight jackets and combat boots, Carhartt T-shirts and Dickies pants.

We ended up at the adult newsstand out of boredom. Mark had borrowed his dad's car for the night, a rusted two-tone Chevy Cavalier nicknamed The Neapolitan. Fred was riding shotgun, which left me in the backseat mosh pit with Charles and Donnie, throwing elbows and doing windmill kicks as Slayer's *Reign in Blood* flooded from the speakers on the back dash. The mosh pit always worried me when Charles was with us. He was a hemophiliac and I couldn't shake the visions of splitting his skin by accident and having to explain to his parents why he bled out in the backseat. To imagine such a scenario wasn't uncommon. My mind often strayed to tragic conclusions, interrupting moments that should have otherwise been carefree. It was a habit that had worsened in recent months.

Our night had started two hours earlier at a 24-hour gas station deep in the suburbs, where I bought a French tickler from a coin-op machine in the bathroom because I thought it was funny, and we all stocked up on Snapple and Reese's peanut butter cups before piling back into the car. Parked at the gas pump closest to the highway, Mark topped off the tank and peeled out onto the highway without paying—The Neapolitan doing its best to accelerate. We all laughed and pounded on the back of Mark's seat while nervously looking out the back window for police lights that never appeared.

We stopped at Conley's Motor Inn first, a budget motel near the mall. It had an indoor pool and waterslide that was infamous because it was rumored that anyone who swam in the pool would develop fungus on their feet. My sister had been invited to birthday parties at Conley's on several occasions throughout grade school, but my mother never let her go. The image of my sister returning home with feet covered in blisters left her too fearful.

Conley's was dead that night, save for the weary travelers arriving by car and those departing by Greyhound, which maintained a small depot in the lodge-like lobby. Motels like this had always piqued my interest. Because of the transient nature of the people in its lobbies, the whole enterprise of a motel was dependent on a temporary agreement between strangers. It was an agreement that brought together a population whose character changed each night at check-in, and turned again at checkout. It was a perpetual game of addition and subtraction, with front desk and custodial staff the only constants.

While none of us had a plan in mind, we each held our breath that we'd discover something fascinating weird, or maybe both. Deep in our hearts I think we all hoped we might stumble upon a group of teenage girls in bikinis swimming in the pool. In a perfect scenario, there would be five girls, one perfectly suited to each of our personalities And if they adored speed metal it would just be an added bonus. I could casually let slip that I was the rhythm guitarist in Mass Affliction, our metal band that had recently played a few shows at the Electric Banana. After sneaking past the front desk and running down the long hallways where hundreds of doors opened onto hundreds of rooms, our hopes were dashed as we arrived at the pool. All we found was a middle-aged couple sitting poolside on a pair of faded chaise longues, nursing drinks from the motel's Hawaiian Lounge.

"We could try to slip into Fairchild's,' Fred said. "I bet there's a party up there." We were back in The Neapolitan, which dutifully chugged along the neon-lit highway. It was cold; the heater in the car barely worked. Fred had turned around in his seat to gauge our interest in his plan.

"Why not?" I said, rubbing my hands together to keep them warm. "Rich people are obviously our crowd." Charles and Donnie both laughed. The cassette in the car's tape deck clicked, switching sides, and the opening riff from "Angel of Death" flooded from the speakers. Mark turned up the radio, which reignited the backseat mosh pit.

Fairchild's was a restaurant in the penthouse suite of an office building that overlooked all of Monroeville. Its logo was written in white-neon script on the side of the building—a callback to midcentury America. It was high-end dining for the rich in the suburbs, people looking for lobster and filet mignon and wine that didn't taste like grape juice. It was a place that loomed large in my imagination.

In the lobby of the building that Fairchild's sat atop, it was quiet as we stepped into the elevator. Mark and Fred were squeezed to one side, Charles, Donnie, and I on the other. I had envisioned it would all be far more glamorous in appearance, like Nakatomi Plaza from *Die Hard*. Instead the smell of stale cigarette smoke hung in the air, and several lights were burned out in the yellowed chandelier illuminating the lobby.

"I bet we get kicked out," Charles said.

"I bet we get drunk," Donnie said.

"I'd be fine with both," I said, laughing.

When the elevator doors opened, you could see all of Monroeville through the restaurant's floor-to-ceiling plate-glass window. It glimmered like a small city in the blackness of night. There were lights from the Miracle Mile and the Turnpike, headlights from cars on the highway and the distant glow of houses on hilltops. I wondered if you could see the mall if you sat in the dining room on the other side of the building, or if the Pittsburgh skyline shimmered on the far horizon. As we stepped off the elevator and into the cocktail lounge, some of the well-dressed patrons already staring, a tall and muscular man wearing a tuxedo greeted us.

"Not tonight, boys," the man said, smiling as he herded us back onto the elevator. "This is a private event." He stepped in with us and pressed the button for the lobby. As the doors slowly closed, the party vanished as quickly as it appeared. No more sounds of smooth jazz or overheard conversation. It was silent in the elevator. None of us spoke. Instead we each watched as the illuminated numbers counted down floor-by-floor.

Without the mall our social life was off-center. We had nowhere to go. It was a reminder of what limited options we had in the suburbs—limitations we came up against all the time. We were too old to languish at home with our parents on New Year's Eve, but too young to be adults. At the mall, our boundaries were better defined. We knew where our adventures started and ended. In the real world, those lines were blurred.

"Happy New Year," said the man in the tuxedo, escorting us through the lobby to the front doors. "Be careful out there."

Before the internet

When my father cut my friends and me loose on Friday nights outside the food court, he gave instructions as to when we should look for his blue Caprice again at the curb. Pick-up time was always the same: nine o'clock. That's when he would circle back for us, while security rooted out the mall rats and groping teenage couples and the burnouts selling weed at the arcade. My father knew I was good for it; that I wouldn't be late because I wanted to come back again.

Before he put the car in drive my friends and I were gone, pushing our way through the double doors and down the escalators that ran on an infinite loop beneath the word "Treats" scribbled in rainbow neon. Past the old timers who lorded over the food court, men dressed in track suits and satin Steelers jackets and velour pullovers who subsisted on coffee and cigarettes and endless free refills at Taco Bell—a Greek chorus commenting on passersby, banging their carpal tunnel wrist braces against the tabletops while bearing nicotine-stained teeth. Some wore sunglasses year round inside and out, others leaned on quad canes and breathed heavy like their lungs were coated in fiberglass.

My friends and I walked with purpose through the food court, past the glass elevator that floated from the first floor to the second floor and back again—ferrying men, women, and children from the intersection outside of Glamour Shots to the heart of the food court. We passed Sbarro and Talk'n Turkey and What's Your Beef, and the glowing cases at Mrs. Fields, where the smell of fresh-baked cookies often lingered until after the lights went dark at closing time. When we reached center court outside of J. C. Penney, where the twin escalators met, we stood among the crowds that flooded the concourse.

Friday night at the mall was always a manic convergence of people from all corners of Pittsburgh's eastern suburbs, with legions of junior high and high school kids flooding through its doors. Teenagers from the small towns in and around the mall—places like Churchill, Wilkinsburg, Penn Hills, Plum, Murrysville, and North Versailles—massed in the concourses, food court, arcade, and parking lots. Jocks in letter jackets roamed the hallways with an air of superiority, team names like Mustangs, Tigers, Gators, and Indians embroidered across their shoulders. Willowy boys with feathered hair, zit-encrusted foreheads, and catfish mustaches stood in clusters near the arcade, stonewashed denim jackets with Megadeth buttons and Nuclear Assault back patches worn with pride. Near the fountain in the food court, girls with bangs teased high, bleach-blonde hair, and purple eye shadow congregated, their jeans skin tight and blouses black and white with sheer sleeves. They all floated in a stream of people that washed through the mall minute-by-minute, hour-by-hour, the white noise so loud it blotted out the sound of the Muzak. Some of the people even spilled outside, where gearheads held court in the parking lot, revving the engines of their restored Chevy Novas and El Caminos and Cutlasses while blue clouds of cigarette smoke hung like exhaust above their heads.

It was a landscape unspoiled by technology, a social network not yet digitized. The mall was the internet before the internet even existed, a cabinet of curiosities for the analog world. I went there to absorb the larger scene unfolding around me—take in the culture I was desperate to consume, understand the people that I saw. It was a place to get lost and learn about music and the rock bands that interested me, to pore over magazines like *Metal Maniacs*, *RIP*, and *Circus*. It was also where I first discovered graphic novels like Alan Moore's *Watchmen* and Frank Miller's *The Dark Knight Returns*, filed on shelves in the back corner at Waldenbooks. Where I escaped into the illustrated realms of *Dungeons & Dragons* manuals, even though I never took on the role of knight or ogre or warlock, or actually played the game. And it was where I first began to take notice of girls.

First kiss

That August, when the phone rang in the kitchen, I didn't expect to hear Sesha's voice on the other end. We hadn't spoken since school let out. Our conversation was brief. She asked if I could meet her at the mall the next day. She was going to be there and would like to see me. I told her I would see her tomorrow, and we hung up. Since I was still too young to drive I had to convince my sister to give me a ride. She would drop me off before her shift at Mr. Steak, where she worked as a waitress.

That next day I met Sesha out front of Tilt, the arcade where her older sister worked, and we walked around the mall for hours. We rode the elevators in Horne's department store. We walked through jewelry and make-up and I bought her a tube of lipstick that she wanted. Sesha asked the worker behind the counter for a tissue so she could wipe away the lipstick she was wearing. I watched as she looked in a small mirror, tightening her lips so she could apply the new color. When she was done she kissed a small piece of white cardboard meant for test sprays of perfume and handed it to me like a business card.

"Thanks for the thoughtful gift," she said.

In the furniture section we sat together on the couches and talked, pretending to live different lives depending on the décor of the room we were in—loud and obnoxious while splayed across a loveseat wrapped in tacky geometric-print fabric; quiet and sophisticated on the black leather couch that seemed destined for delivery to a psychologist's office. On one of the last couches Sesha took my hand and held it in her lap, playing with my fingers as she talked. She was wearing cut-off jean shorts and the white of her pockets peeked out a little at the bottom; the back of my hand rested against the warm skin on her upper thigh. It was strange to be sitting with Sesha. We hadn't spoken in almost three months, since school let out, yet we were acting like boyfriend and girlfriend.

As I walked Sesha back to the arcade where her sister worked, we held hands. School would be starting in a couple weeks. We made small talk, wondering which teachers we might have and what subjects we hoped to take. I wasn't looking forward to going back. When we reached the arcade I could see Sesha's sister in the back. She stood behind a glass display case teeming with prizes meticulously organized in colored plastic bins. Teenagers stood in clusters around Street Fighter and Mortal Kombat arcade games, their faces lit by screen glow. As I was about to turn and walk away, Sesha leaned in and kissed me on the lips. It caught me by surprise, and my whole body seemed to vibrate. "Call me tonight," she said with a smile, before vanishing into the arcade.

The mall as ritual

With my T-shirt in a ball on the bedroom floor, and my left arm extended to the ceiling, I recited a sequence of numbers in my head: *One, two, three, four, five, six.* A single swipe of deodorant accompanied each number in the silent count. If the swipes were inconsistent, I had to start over. Like if the edge of the plastic deodorant stick container scratched against my skin, or if one swipe felt longer than the other. Whenever the sequence got interrupted I would fret until I made it right. It was a ritual, and it had a prescribed order.

By the time I heard the rattling engine of Edward's gold Chevette out in the driveway, it was too late to stop the dog. Kelly was already howling, disturbed from her nap at the foot of my bed, her milk-polished eyes and gray muzzle pointed at the ceiling while a patch of fur on the back of her neck stood on end. Edward pounded on the horn in the center of his steering wheel and it let out a series of dull, stuttering drones.

"Out in a minute," I yelled from my bedroom window at the back of the house. Kelly hurried from the room to investigate the noise. From the corner of my eye I saw her jump from the bed, heard the nails on her paws click-clacking as she walked across the hardwood floor in the living room on her way to the front door, where she let out another howl. Edward and I were headed to Kmart to shoplift spray paint, then over to the mall to eat tacos in the food court. It was a ritual we observed several times a week. One that never grew old no matter how many times we repeated it. Our trips to the mall forced me out of the house, out of my room. I came to depend on them.

I ran into the bathroom, wet a washcloth with warm water, and wiped away large white clumps of deodorant from under each armpit. I would have to start over. But the skin was raw and irritated, and Edward was out front waiting. My forehead started to sweat. Last thing I wanted was for him to walk in the house and catch me in the middle of whatever this was. It was too embarrassing. He'd find me shirtless, with violent red streaks extending from under the bicep on each arm to the top of my ribcage. Edward knew about my OCD. All of my friends did. But it was more of an oddity to them, almost a joke. My quirks often acted as comic relief. I never went out of my way to talk about how debilitating the disorder had become.

Back in my bedroom I settled on a compromise, a silent three count: *One, two, three.* It would have to do. The antidepressants that I took each morning, a cocktail of serotonin reuptake inhibitors, freed my brain enough to allow shortcuts. Still, altering the ritual always left me unsettled. It required trust that nothing cataclysmic would happen, a belief that I used to will myself out the door. I laced up an old pair of black-and-white Vans and threw on a teal hooded sweatshirt that had become a favorite of mine. I ran past Kelly on my way out the door, patting her on the head before bounding down the front lawn toward Edward's gold Chevette.

Outside of my friendships and the peace I found at the mall, the last year had been difficult for my family. Since freshman year of high school, my mood and state of mind had started to shift. I spent more time by myself; I slept long hours and was impossible to wake in the mornings; and I was regularly acting out of character—a change most noticeably marked by fits of anger and near-constant irritability with everyone around me. The most dramatic changes, however, were a series of compulsive and increasingly odd behaviors. I had taken to constantly checking door locks, excessively washing my hands, counting every footstep that I took, and had even developed an overwhelming concern that each time I spoke I might offend someone. It was maddening.

When I lingered on these behaviors, I would attempt to trace them back to a source. I remembered how, as a young boy, I used to count my footsteps and pattern the way I walked to suit those numbers. Sets of three or four, avoiding cracks in sidewalks, ascending staircases two steps at a time. Was that normal behavior, or were those rituals in their infancy? If I failed to observe the numbers, I imagined something bad might happen. But it was a nebulous fear—quiet but unformed. By the time I was a teenager that fear metastasized, its form heavy and defined in my thoughts. I often returned to a particular afternoon from the second summer after we moved to Regency Park, when Robert Magaro beat the shit out of me while I was delivering newspapers. He claimed I had made fun of him behind his back. It wasn't true, but that didn't matter. He terrorized me that summer—chasing me down, threatening more violence, whispering to anyone who would listen that he better not see me around the neighborhood, or else. After that I began to obsess over what I said, how I said it, and whom I said it to.

My erratic behavior and the weight of my new habits had my parents concerned. So after months of resisting, I had finally agreed to an evaluation at Western Psychiatric Institute and Clinic. In December of 1992, just a few weeks before Christmas, I was formally diagnosed with severe clinical depression and obsessive-compulsive disorder. It proved that my parent's fears were not unfounded. Something was wrong with me.

The quiet presence of the mall gave order to my life. The smell of soft pretzels wafting from the food court summoned dopamine in my brain, while the terrazzo beneath my feet afforded at least a temporary stability.

It was an environment of predictable familiarity. The mall offered things I could count on—from landmarks like the grand fountain outside of Horne's department store, where I often got lost in a Zen-like calm as I watched the blue-tinted water reach skyward, to the euphoric rush of running the secret hallways that spread out like a network of arteries behind the storefronts. The mall allowed me the space to step away from my obsessions, rituals, and the troubling thoughts that increasingly dogged me. And it let me feel like a normal teenager for a few short hours.

9 YOUNG LOVE

"What are you knuckleheads up to?" Michelle said, happy to see us. She was standing across from Charles and I in the upper level of the mall, near where the clock tower used to rise from the courtyard outside of Kaufmann's. We had been wandering the hallways when we bumped into Michelle. She was nineteen, two years older than me, and home for the weekend from Indiana University of Pennsylvania, where she was a freshman. She had come to the mall that night to pick up applications for a summer job.

"We are doing absolutely nothing," I said, widening my eyes to stress the level of boredom we were experiencing. "I mean *nothing*."

"Help me find a job," Michelle said, revealing two small dimples on her cheeks when she smiled. "Please don't make me do it alone." Her brown eyes and full lips were striking, the way she carried herself too.

It was a Friday night in May of 1994; the mall was crawling with people. Charles and I walked with Michelle as she collected applications at Contempo and then the Gap, before heading to the food court, where part-time work was always available. At Sbarro, Michelle stood across the counter from a thin, silver-haired man with a desperate expression on his face. He was the manager. I recognized him from my endless days seated at a table near Taco Bell, where I survived on a steady diet of bean burritos and free refills. The man was animated as he spoke, arms waving as his bottlebrush mustache bounced in rhythm with his words. He watched optimistically as Michelle walked away, application in hand.

"Whoa," she whispered as she walked back to the table in the food court where Charles and I were sitting. "That guy was about to pull me behind the counter and put me to work." We talked as she filled in her name and social security number on the application. It had been photocopied so many times that some of the words were indecipherable and the blank lines nothing but bent squiggles. As Charles stepped away to order tacos, I asked Michelle what college was like. I was curious if school got any better when you were farther away from home.

I knew Michelle from high school; there was overlap in our circle of friends. But other than dancing with her once at a Christmas dance held in the high school cafeteria, where janitors had folded up the lunch tables and pushed them to the side, we had never talked much. I was aware of her, though. Michelle, with her dyed red hair cut short in a bob, was hard to miss. She was a fixture in the hallways of our suburban high school, a monolithic building tucked among dairy farms and cow pastures. As she strolled with her friends she always seemed to be having so much fun. And her collection of concert T-shirts always piqued my interest: Violent Femmes, Lemonheads, Morrissey, Sonic Youth.

Michelle was friendly with everyone in the large, loosely connected group of art kids, skateboarders, goth girls, and metalheads that we each associated with. She had a way with people that I admired—it was so much different than my own way of handling the world. It was Michelle I thought of when I imagined the kind of girl I wanted to date. She was kind, funny, and independent, but also lacked any pretension.

"Where are you guys headed after this?" Michelle asked, folding her completed application in half.

"I have to get home," Charles said, reflexively tucking his long dark hair behind his ears. "But Matt has nowhere to be."

"Thanks," I said. "That barely makes me sound pathetic."

"Friends of mine are having a party in Oakland, down at Carnegie Mellon," Michelle said. "I was planning to stop by, if you'd like to come."

"Sure," I said, excited at the invitation.

As we left the food court, Michelle handed her application to the thin, silver-haired man behind the counter at Sbarro. Reaching the escalators, we slowly floated from the first floor to the second, the rainbow neon above us glowing like firelight. On our way up I noticed the Two Jasons, a pair of older teens with mustaches who often antagonized me. One of them mouthed the familiar phrase "fuck you faggot" as they passed. I smiled and waved as always. We parted ways with Charles at the top. Michelle and I talked as we walked out to the parking lot together, the towering lamplights shining down on us.

* * *

I was working at a Holiday Inn near the Pennsylvania Turnpike in Monroeville when I met Michelle, washing dishes in the kitchen of a karaoke bar called The Cheatin' Heart Saloon. It was a dive bar for disenfranchised suburbanites—drunks singing Garth Brooks and Clint Black songs into a beer-soaked microphone; men and women dressed in their best acid-washed denim purchased at the mall; a revolving door of belligerent alcoholics; and overpriced bar food prepared by an assemblage of down-on-their-luck cooks. It was a thankless, bottom-rung job. But I didn't work there because it paid well or offered a promising future. I washed dirty dishes to fulfill a promise.

In March of 1994, as part of an agreement with my parents, I quit high school. But the deal came with two stipulations: I had to find a part-time job and I had to begin studying for my GED. So toward the end of my junior year, two months after my seventeenth birthday, I dropped out. It was a decision more pragmatic than reckless. Severe clinical depression and obsessive-compulsive disorder had deeply disrupted my life since freshman year. Those issues, alongside bitter feuding with teachers, suspensions, fighting with other students, run-ins with police, and frequent absences, had all but destroyed my academic record, leaving me perpetually behind. I was young and overwhelmed, and, at the time, breaking free from school seemed more realistic than the prospect that I could somehow magically fix it all.

Aside from a surprisingly small amount of money, my job at the hotel provided a simple structure to my weeks. I would work three or four weeknights and almost every Friday and Saturday, usually getting home a little before midnight. Most mornings I woke late and ate Lucky Charms to soothe the acid reflux caused by my antidepressants, played guitar for hours, and watched cartoons until my brain hurt. In the window of time between the end of the school day and when I had to start work, I sometimes saw friends as they arrived home. On good days my friends would skip school so we could all hang out together. We'd drive downtown to Eide's and buy tapes and comic books, the same ritual we observed before I dropped out. On my nights off from work I attended my GED prep course at a nearby community college, taught by a high school teacher who was moonlighting for extra cash and seemed indifferent about his students' prospects for the future.

When I wasn't washing dishes at the Holiday Inn, or languishing in a community college classroom, I spent all of my time at the mall—more than I ever had in my life. Walking the concourses. Slipping off to the secret passageways behind the stores. Shoplifting whatever I wanted as a way to feel some sense of control. Accompanied by friends at times, but often I was alone. The mall remained a constant amid personal turmoil; a place to escape that wasn't my job or the basement bedroom at my parent's house. While leaving high school behind offered a chance to start over, it was a decision that weighed on me. I was a high school dropout washing dishes at a Holiday Inn. I wondered if I had made a terrible mistake.

* * *

By the time Michelle parked her grandmother's gray Buick Skylark outside of my parent's house in Regency Park, it was after midnight. The warm spring air had turned cool; a nearby streetlight illuminating the dew-dotted grass of the front yard. The party we had gone to at Carnegie Mellon was still going on when we left. But I had work the next morning, and Michelle needed to get her grandmother's car back home.

It was quiet in the Skylark with the engine turned off. I had been thinking of what to say to Michelle, how to thank her for taking me along. I didn't want to sound foolish, but spending time with her made me feel better than I had in months. And it was more than just her fun, carefree attitude; there was lightness between us that allowed me to be myself. It felt like a burden had been lifted from my shoulders. I didn't want to say goodbye.

"Would you like to come inside for a minute?" I asked, nervously.

"Sure," Michelle said, smiling as she pulled the keys from the ignition. "I should just get back soon so my grandmother doesn't kill me."

After closing the car doors, we both stood in the shadow of a tall pine. As she walked toward me, I stepped closer before leaning in to kiss her. Michelle paused for a moment, then put her hands on my cheeks as we kissed. We looked at each other for a moment after. Something was happening that I couldn't explain. I took her hand and led her up the front lawn toward the house. Slowly opening the front door, careful not to wake anyone, we snuck inside. The lights were on in the kitchen, and I could hear the low hum of the TV in my parent's bedroom. We walked toward the sink and stood together, leaning against the Formica countertop.

"Are you thirsty?" I asked. "Would you like some orange juice?"

"That would be nice," Michelle said.

I opened the refrigerator and reached for a carton of Tropicana, then grabbed two small juice glasses from the cabinet above the sink.

"Now with more pulp," I said, repeating a phrase printed in bold type on the carton.

"Wow," Michelle said, chuckling a little.

As we stood there drinking orange juice, we joked that there was so much pulp we had to use our front teeth to filter it all out. Hearing the noise of our conversation, Kelly appeared from the back bedroom on watchdog duty, slower than usual but curious about this new person. She cautiously greeted us, and Michelle kneeled down to softly pet the brown-and-black fur on the top of her head. Before Michelle had to leave we talked a few minutes longer, Kelly looking back and forth between us, and I felt more whole than I had in years.

Sometimes still, when I stand in front of an illuminated cooler case at the grocery store, I see the pulpy orange juice and think of that first night we met. Often it's because Michelle has texted me on my way home from work and asked that I pick up a few things for our sons' school lunches. Usually its apples, bananas, yogurt, and string cheese on my list. But sometimes I go in search of orange juice, no pulp.

PART THREE

ADULTHOOD

10 HOMECOMING

As the mall's automatic doors closed behind me the Muzak seemed to swell. A digitized rendition of Chuck Mangione's "Feels So Good" scored the movements of the strangers coming and going around me. Some moved in lockstep with the beat while others appeared to be tuned in to an alternate frequency. Past a bank of vending machines and a skill crane teeming with colorful prizes, I stopped when I reached the end court outside of Macy's. I watched as pairs and trios and quartets of people walked beneath the sun-pierced skylights in the mall's promenade—men and women, women and women, men and men. These people weren't shopping; the mall wasn't open yet. They were mall walkers—tracing invisible routes on the terrazzo—accruing miles lap by lap. What drew me to the mall that morning, though different in motive, was similarly ritualistic.

It was June of 2009 and I had just lost my job as a magazine editor the day before, having learned during a brief phone call that my position no longer existed. I was with Michelle and our two-year-old son when I got the news, on vacation at a cabin in Pennsylvania's Laurel Highlands. The company where I worked had been laying off employees since the stock market crash in October of the previous year. While I had survived two rounds of downsizing, the cuts finally caught up to me. That morning, before ending up at the mall, I had driven forty miles west to my former employer so that I could clean out my cubicle.

It was early when I arrived, just before 7:00 a.m., and the magazine offices were almost vacant. Sound barely registered in the building, save for the hum of a thousand florescent overhead lights. A stack of empty boxes had been left on my desk, but everything else looked the same as how I left it. Sandy from human resources, who had escorted me from the entrance of the building to my cubicle—confiscating my company laptop, cell phone, and security key along the way—gave me a sympathetic look, her head tilted to the side. "Take all the time you need," she said. "I'll check back with you in about 10 minutes."

Other than my personal belongings and a few professional mementos not much was worth saving, and before long I was back in my car with nowhere to go. To my right, cradled in the passenger seat, was a Hammermill paper box filled with framed photographs, artwork from my two-year-old son, a pencil holder I received as a Christmas gift one year, and my diploma from the University of Pittsburgh. More boxes were stashed in the back. One wedged in my son's empty car seat, the other resting on the floor. Each contained memories—paperwork, press kits, media passes, and other assorted trinkets—collected during my five-year tenure at the magazine. All of it seemed out of place in my Honda Civic.

That morning, I arrived at Monroeville Mall by instinct. Not because I had an errand to run, or because I was particularly eager to spend money. I was searching for something. A place to belong, or at least where I once belonged. After all that happened that morning I wanted to feel safe, to rediscover the magic I felt in that mall as a small child. I wanted to see if that sense of wonder was still within reach.

"A child's world is fresh and new and beautiful, full of wonder and excitement," Rachel Carson wrote in 1956. "It is our misfortune that for most of us that clear-eyed vision, that true instinct for what is beautiful and awe-inspiring, is dimmed and even lost before we reach adulthood."[1]

If turmoil during my teenage years had dimmed my clear-eyed vision, the burden of work as an adult had most certainly burned it out. At the mall, I wondered if finding a way back was even possible. Could reentry in a familiar place rekindle the joy and curiosity I once felt?

My emotional connection to the mall has always been difficult to quantify. In *Dawn of the Dead*, when the four main characters discover the mall and see it as a potential sanctuary, they land their helicopter on the roof to investigate. As they look for a way in, there's a tender exchange between Stephen and Francine, who are romantically involved, as they peer through the skylights at the undead shoppers shuffling in the concourses and promenades below.

"What are they doing? Why do they come here?" she asks.

"Some kind of instinct. Memory of what they used to do," Stephen replies. "This was an important place in their lives."

Up and down the concourses store clerks were still unlocking the security gates—from Foot Locker to Bath & Body Works, Hot Topic to Victoria's Secret—florescent tube lights popping on row after row above their heads. As I walked, I noticed a painting in an illuminated storefront window. It depicted a rustic cabin in a lush valley. A distant mountain range towered behind it, the leaves on the trees tinted orange and crimson to signify the change of season, while a stream gushed in the foreground. Painted by Thomas Kinkade, resident artist at hundreds of shopping malls across the country, it was by no means high art. But as I stared into that painting a calm washed over me. It reminded me yet again of the strange and unexpected peace that I've found at the mall throughout my life. Since I first walked these hallways as a child, hand-in-hand with my mother and father, to the endless days spent breathing the mall's recycled air as a teenager. But now none of that felt like it had ever even happened. Or if it did, it was a time so far removed from my present self that it no longer seemed real.

Days later, at a bar, I would tell my friend Mike that I wanted to make a short film about mall walkers. How there was a mesmerizing choreography to it all, the way the old timers and retirees and soccer moms circled the upper and lower levels each morning, occasionally stopping to talk or break for coffee, and how the whole ritual would reset the next day. I wanted to immerse myself in that ritual, somehow make that moment that I experienced mean something.

For years Mike and I had made a habit of daydreaming out loud, particularly when alcohol was involved. Our plans were aspirational. Mike might wax poetic about starting a T-shirt line inspired by popular phrases pulled from nineties-era hip-hop songs, while, moments later, also entertaining the possibility of opening a shoe store that dealt only in rare, hard-to-find brands. But as more alcohol seeped into our bloodstreams we often became introspective, confessing that we had no surefire plans to realize any of our ideas. Except this time was different. I was no longer a teenager with no responsibilities, or even a recent college graduate with little to lose. I was thirty-two years old, a husband and father, and woefully unemployed. I needed to learn how to live again.

While my life had changed, so too had the mall. Gone were the tropical gardens, fountains, and lava rock waterfalls that electrified my imagination as a child. In their place, teeth-whitening booths and Proactiv Acne Solution kiosks dotted the concourse. Gone too was the Ice Palace skating rink. My father often took me there on Saturdays to watch the ice skaters circle the rink, though we never ventured out on the ice ourselves. It's where Alex Owens, the protagonist in *Flashdance* (1983), watched as her friend Jeanie Szabo had her professional figure skating dreams dashed as she tumbled to the ice over and over again—her heartbreak choreographed to Laura Branigan's "Gloria." Also missing from the landscape was the towering Clock of Nations, which no longer chimed each hour as shoppers streamed in and out of Gimbels. In its place an empty end court and a shuttered Boscov's. All that remained of that distant wonderland was a small footbridge that overlooked a goldfish pond.

Euphoria is not uncommon at the mall—even for adults who are expected to know better. Small children experience it each time they pass a cluster of coin-operated rides in an atrium or end court. To see rocket ships, motorcycles, safari jeeps, and military helicopters all shrunken to scale is an open invitation. To this day, when I see an old red-and-white merry-go-round outside of a Kmart I feel a pang of nostalgia for my own childhood. I remember the tinny carnival music that played from a speaker embedded in the red-coated fiberglass canopy, and my mother's smile.

At center court in the mall, where the twin escalators meet, I paused at the coin-operated rides. My two-year-old son is particularly fond of the ice cream truck at the mall, and I see myself in his joy. He never even cares if I bring the truck to life with the coins in my pocket. He is enthralled, simply enough, at the power of becoming the ice cream man. We are both men in that moment. He takes my order and I pay him in imaginary money. Seconds later, he hands me an invisible ice cream cone topped with my favorite flavor. Sometimes he gives me imaginary change. It's a magical transaction. And when our business is done, we return home.

11 GHOST MALLS

There are no unsacred places; there are only sacred places and desecrated places.

—WENDELL BERRY

When demolition crews arrived at Greengate Mall in May 2003, it marked the end of a decade-long financial collapse that had left the shopping mall in a state of obsolescence. Shuttered two years earlier, the vacant mall—a community fixture in and around the town of Greensburg, Pennsylvania, for nearly 40 years—was being razed to make way for a Walmart Supercenter. News of the demolition upset longtime customers and former employees, senior citizens who walked the concourses for morning exercise and former mall rats who came of age in Greengate's neon hallways. Losing the mall also triggered an almost immediate sense of longing among those who adored it.

"It wasn't just a place to shop," said Gary Nelson. "It was a community center." Nelson, who was born in the late 1980s, grew up going to Greengate. It was the mall his parents preferred. Before his family had a car, they would take a bus to the mall from where they lived in the nearby town of Jeannette. When asked to recall his most vivid memories of Greengate, Nelson cited dinners at Elby's, playing video games at Tilt, and shopping at stores like G. C. Murphy and National Record Mart. His family's trips to the mall, much like my own as a child, were experiences steeped in emotion.

"Walking through those doors, I remember the distinct smell of the perfume department," Nelson said. "As we walked through the store and into the upper floor of the mall, the whooshing sound from the 30-foot-high fountain could be heard throughout the entire indoor courtyard."

Greengate Mall first opened its doors in August 1965. Developed by James W. Rouse and designed by Victor Gruen, the mall featured all the requisite charm of a midcentury shopping center—decorative fountains, skylights, lush plant life, pastel birdcages, and benches dotting the thoroughfares. Situated at the gateway to the Laurel Highlands, a stretch of mountainous terrain located an hour east of Pittsburgh, Pennsylvania, it became a rural retail oasis—serving as a de facto town square among the area's farmland and early postwar suburban developments. When a shopping mall is shuttered, particularly one as adored as Greengate, its community is not only displaced—they are fragmented.

"It was like a small town where everyone knew one another," Nelson said of Greengate, referring not only to the people who worked there, but mall regulars too. In 2004, as a response to the void left by the closure of the mall, Nelson started a website called Greengate Mall Revisited. The site acted as an online time capsule to preserve the memory of the mall through photographs, videos, ephemera, and discussion. In 2011 much of the activity moved to Facebook, where Nelson started a public group as a hub for ex-Greengaters. Nearly two decades after the mall was demolished, the group continues to serve as memorial and scrapbook, forum and therapy session. The comments read like an overheard conversation among old friends.

"Loved that mall," Sheri McDonald wrote in response to a photograph of Greengate's food court from the early 1990s. "I was always there with friends on Fridays and Saturdays. Great memories!" In the photograph, the entrance to Montgomery Ward is visible and a slender, blonde-haired woman wearing a red apron stands in the foreground, broom and dustpan in hand. People are everywhere around her. Sitting at tables and walking the concourses lined with neon-lit storefronts. "No mall could ever replace Greengate," wrote Kim Jo Golack. "Loved hanging with Terry Ranieri and they had the best Christmas displays." When Faith Hall Baker chimed in, her sentiment punctuated the discussion: "Liked it better than any of the malls!"

Online eulogies for America's vacant shopping malls are nothing new. Deadmalls.com, for example, the oft-cited authority on the ill-fated pleasure domes that dot the fifty states, has been operating since the turn of the century, going live as the rampant fear over Y2K still lingered in the nation's collective memory. And while the legions of shuttered malls filed in the site's archives have only grown larger over the last two decades, the practice of photographing and reminiscing about the dead or dying malls where many of us spent our youth has become a rather ubiquitous form of shared nostalgia in our online lives. For those whose childhood malls either no longer exist, sit empty, or teeter on the brink of closure, it acts as a form of catharsis.

In April 2014, after BuzzFeed published an article laden with images of abandoned malls from across the country, I noticed how the comments section became a much-needed emotional outlet for many readers. One woman, commenting on the derelict state of Rolling Acres Mall in Akron, Ohio, shared a particularly evocative memory.

"This is where I spent my childhood," she wrote. "I made my first wish with a penny in a fountain here, played pinball in the arcade—Aladdin's Castle—with my dad. My ears were pierced here, it's where I saw my first movie, and I still crave the hush puppies and gyros sold in the food court. I came with my whole family here. Sat on Santa's lap. I encountered the mystery of plasma globes and learned to see with the 'magic eye.' I would marvel at the massive palm trees and dream of going to Florida someday to see them in the wild—dead fronds of one is pictured in the fourth photo down, taken just beside the glass elevator that I always longed to ride up and down, as if teleporting. It became a central place for gang activity in the '90s, leading to the eventual closing. I am not sad that this is its fate—I am sad that this was the landscape of my childhood in the first place, and that it's impermanence can bring me to tears."[1]

The woman's final sentiment, the acknowledgment that a shopping mall in suburban Ohio may not have been the ideal place to spend her childhood, is bittersweet. All of her emotions seemed to bubble to the surface as she typed, leading to that moment of recognition. Prefaced by such sweet recollections of time spent with her father, and the awe and wonder of experiencing the mall through the eyes of a child, it's intriguing that as an adult she feels such regret. A certain language of loss pervades her words, a reckoning that deems the shopping mall an unsatisfactory place in her personal history. She sounds almost mournful—not only for the loss of the mall, but for the childhood she wished she had.

When Rolling Acres closed in 2008, the country was already slipping into the disquiet of the Great Recession. Banks were falling apart, American automakers were insolvent, and shopping malls were no longer being built. Even though Akron's boom years were well behind it when the recession hit, Rolling Acres became a cautionary tale. A dead mall languishing in Northeast Ohio's flat and endless landscape, once a vibrant swath of the American Rust Belt, symbolized fading fortunes on a grand scale. Since then the mall has become a pilgrimage site for those who want to pay their respects—not only to the mall itself, but what it represented in their lives. Some are visitors who frequented the mall in its prime, whether as children, teenagers, or adults. Others are outsiders—urban explorers, mall enthusiasts, curious strangers—who have heard of the mall's derelict condition and feel a need or desire to bear witness.

Photographer Tag Christof represents the latter. His curiosity has drawn him to Rolling Acres time and again in recent years. When asked what it is that brings him back, his response borders on poetic. "I'm looking for subtle signifiers of an exuberant bygone optimism," he said. "Whether people realize it or not, the things I photograph are the direct result of a system that defines progress only in economic terms." Born in New Mexico in the 1980s, Christof, who grew up visiting Villa Linda Mall in Santa Fe and Coronado Mall in Albuquerque, has spent the last five years crisscrossing the country in an effort to document architectural sites vanishing from the landscape. While his photographic project, dubbed *America is Dead*, doesn't focus exclusively on shopping malls, they play a prominent part in illustrating his view of an America that no longer exists.

Unlike other photographers who frequent dead malls, particularly those who traffic in the type of ruin porn that dominates the internet—feeding a growing public obsession with real-world dystopian landscapes—Christof's approach is far more measured. Often shot with a Bronica medium format camera loaded with Kodak Portra film, his photographs are imbued with lush color and natural light that temporarily resuscitate the hallways, storefronts, and entrances of deserted malls like Rolling Acres. One image from a recent trip to the mall captures the label-scarred facade of a department store bathed in golden sunlight as evening approaches. Towering light posts stand like quiet sentinels in the foreground, while overgrown pines cast shadows against painted white brick. In another of Christof's photographs, this one taken in the food court at Canton Centre Mall in nearby Canton, Ohio, an Orange Julius sits empty but alive, so much so that you can almost envision a line of teenagers queued at the counter.

Viewed together, Christof's images offer an ode to American aspiration and its rewards, tempered by the reality of what happens when economies fail and people stop buying. Each photograph is as much about the past as it is about the present and future, as much about what happens before a photo is taken, as it is about what happens after. Maybe that's because Christof's ethos is akin to photographers like Stephen Shore or Robert Adams, whose affinity for American landscapes and quotidian scenes show reverence for the common places that become sacred in our lives. He also approaches his work with a deep interest in not only the place he is photographing, but also the people to whom it mattered. In the many conversations he's had with strangers outside of dead or dying shopping malls, Christof has discovered that his role is as much about looking as it is listening. Rolling Acres is no exception.

"People recall celebrity visits, holiday decorations, beautiful carousels, awkward first dates, their first splurge purchases, first jobs, and saving their allowances to buy something from a resplendent toy store," he said. "Most talk about how, by the late 1990s and mid-2000s, they just stopped going there."

To describe these shopping malls as dead is almost unfair. Certainly they no longer function as intended; there are no more products on display or commodities available for purchase. If anything, these vacant malls have entered a new phase, one where trees take root in cracked floor tiles and feral cats pass unnoticed—where curiosity seekers find meaning in the afterlife of a place that has long outlived its original intent. These are the ghost malls, places where past, present, and future simultaneously collapsed.

Ghost malls like Rolling Acres dot the country. In Northeast Ohio alone, there is Euclid Square Mall, Randall Park Mall, and Canton Centre Mall. To speak the names of shopping malls where the lights have permanently gone dark is like reciting an incantation: Cloverleaf Mall in Chesterfield, Virginia; North Towne Square Mall in Toledo, Ohio; Woodville Mall in Northwood, Ohio; Crestwood Mall in St. Louis, Missouri; Hawthorne Plaza Mall in Hawthorne, California; Dixie Square Mall in Harvey, Illinois; Turfland Mall in Lexington, Kentucky; and Greengate Mall in Greensburg, Pennsylvania.

No mall is forever; their lifespan, like our own, is finite.

12 UTOPIA INTERRUPTED

Wherever people feel safe . . . they will be indifferent.
—SUSAN SONTAG, *REGARDING THE PAIN OF OTHERS*

On a cold Saturday night, one week before Valentines' Day, seventeen-year-old Tarod Thornhill entered the lower level of Macy's department store in Monroeville Mall, semiautomatic handgun at his side, and opened fire. It was early evening, around 7:30 p.m., and the store was crowded. So too was the mall, with hundreds of shoppers in the concourses and end courts, including dozens of small children in the nearby Mister Rogers Neighborhood playground.

When Thornhill pulled the trigger he fired five shots. His intended target, twenty-year-old Davon Jones, was struck by three of those bullets and critically injured, with gunshot wounds to his left flank, pelvic region, and left buttock. At the same time, Thomas Singleton, his wife Mary, and their twelve-year-old son Dylan walked by. Singleton, who passed beside Jones just as Thornhill opened fired, was shot in the back of his left leg, severing his femoral artery. Mary Singleton was shot in her left shoulder. Their son Dylan, only a couple steps behind them, was not struck.

As the gunfire rang out, shoppers stampeded from the men's department, flooding into the mall to escape immediate danger and seek shelter. Thornhill ran into the mall as well, swept up in the rush. Surveillance footage captured the scene in its entirety. In the video Thornhill can be seen greeting a small group of friends. They briefly talk to each other, even smile and laugh. But a moment later, as they all begin to walk, Thornhill's arm is extended and he's holding a gun as he fires into the crowd, with Jones recoiling first, and Thomas and Mary Singleton each falling to the ground seconds later. Muzzle flashes, which are visible in the video, violently punctuate each gunshot. Running backward as he shoots, Thornhill disappears out of frame and into the mall.

"We were down by Aunt Anne's pretzels and then we just heard all these gunshots," a young woman told WTAE News that night. "We didn't see anyone running at first, we just heard all these screams." Another eyewitness, who was shopping with her teenage daughter when Thornhill opened fire, recalled fleeing to safety: "I heard the shots—pop, pop, pop—and I snatched my daughter . . . we ran to the back of the store, heard another round of shots go off, and we locked ourselves in the bathroom."

The mall was placed on lockdown. Clerks closed storefront security gates and hid with shoppers in stock rooms and storage closets. Mall security stood guard at all exits. Monroeville Police arrived in force, dressed in flak jackets and armed with assault rifles, going store by store to evacuate the mall before closing early. News vans converged on the Macy's parking lot as reporters prepared to broadcast the aftermath of the shooting on live television. By that point, word of the incident had already spread to social media.

"Just saw 2 ppl get shot. They are letting guns go in there," Kansas City Chiefs quarterback Terrelle Pryor posted on Twitter. "10 more shots went off and was getting closer to me." Pryor, who grew up in the nearby town of Jeannette, just happened to be at the mall that night when the gunfire broke out.

Thornhill was arrested hours later at his home in Brackenridge. Police were able to identify him using a photograph he posted to his Instagram account earlier that night, in which he was wearing a hooded sweatshirt that matched what police saw in the surveillance video. Thornhill also had a prior record from an incident in 2012, when at age fourteen he stole a Jeep Cherokee and led police on a high-speed chase that ended when he crashed the car and was arrested.

That night's shooting wasn't the first time Monroeville Mall had made news in recent months. Six weeks earlier, a riot had broken out at the mall. Initial reports on social media claimed it was a Black Lives Matter protest, mirroring similar demonstrations across the country following the deaths of Michael Brown in Ferguson, Missouri; Eric Garner in Staten

Island, New York; and Tamir Rice in Cleveland, Ohio, all at the hands of police. But those early reports were false.

It turned out that over a thousand teenagers had massed in the first-floor concourses, not to protest or to demonstrate, but to incite violence. As dozens of fistfights broke out, the situation quickly escalated, with frequent altercations taking place over a three-hour period; iPhone videos from that night captured the mall in a state of chaos. One video showed a teenage girl being beaten—slapped, punched, kicked, hair pulled—as several teenage girls ganged up on her. Another video showed similar scenarios unfolding simultaneously, with mall security unable to calm the crowds. By the time police had control of the situation, several teenagers had been seriously injured and rushed to nearby hospitals.

In the nearly fifty years since Monroeville Mall first opened, the world has changed dramatically. Malls no longer occupy the same space in our collective imagination. And for a large swath of the population, they no longer serve the same purposes either. In many regards, shopping malls have become faded monuments to the aspirations of post–Second World War Americans. When the first malls were built in the mid-1950s by men like Victor Gruen, James Rouse, and A. Alfred Taubman they were viewed as utopic interventions in the banal landscape of suburban America. These new crystal palaces would solve the problem of social isolation by recreating the town square. People would find what they needed to buy, but they would also find friendship and conversation. As a concept, it had a lot to live up to. But since then, circumstances have changed. Today the suburban dream, which once featured the mall as its centerpiece, has become a nightmare for so many. In the wake of the Great Recession, mortgage foreclosures, and record unemployment, low-income residents and the middle class are still struggling to recover from all that they lost. And the problems that led so many to flee from cities in the 1950s and 1960s—crime, drugs, poverty, and blight—have long existed in the suburbs. Still the mall remains a symbol—for better or worse—of American optimism, and American excess too.

In recent years, malls across the country have experienced an increase in violence, from terroristic threats to mass shootings to stabbings. In February of 2015, Al Shabaab, a jihadist terrorist group from East Africa, ordered an attack on the Mall of America in an online video. As the masked narrator speaks, graphic imagery from the Westgate Mall killings in Nairobi, Kenya, in 2013—which left sixty people dead—is used to illustrate his threats. Three years earlier, 24-year-old James Holmes walked into a movie theater at Town Center at Aurora in Aurora, Colorado, and opened fire, killing twelve and wounding fifty-eight during a screening of *The Dark Knight Rises*. It was the deadliest shooting in Colorado since the Columbine High School massacre in 1999.

On September 17, 2016, a mass stabbing took place at Crossroads Center in St. Cloud, Minnesota. The attacker was 22-year-old Dahir A. Adan. Armed with two steak knives, he began stabbing shoppers outside the mall before moving inside, where he was shot multiple times during a confrontation with an off-duty police officer. Ten people were injured in the stabbing, but no motive for the attacks was ever reported. Less than a week later, five people were killed in a mass shooting at the Cascade Mall in Burlington, Washington. Four women and one man were among the dead. The gunman was identified as Arcan Cetin, a twenty-year-old who emigrated from Turkey as a child with his family. He escaped the mall that night but was arrested the next day.

Shopping malls have also become an unlikely site for political action—from peaceful protests to civil disobedience. In December of 2014, some 2,000 Black Lives Matter demonstrators filled the rotunda at the Mall of America in Bloomington, Minnesota, chanting: "While you're on your shopping spree, black people cannot breathe." The protest was a response to the recent nationwide deaths of young black men at the hands of police. A year later protests erupted again at the Mall of America, this time following the killing of Jamar Clark, a 24-year-old unarmed black man who was shot by Minneapolis Police. For weeks, demonstrators had demanded to know the names of the officers involved in the shooting and requested that the department release surveillance footage of the incident.

These protests highlighted the ever-increasing divide between law enforcement and the black community, and ignited nationwide criticisms about the appropriate use of force. As the demonstration at the Mall of America made national news, rapper and activist Talib Kweli posted a photograph to Instagram showing dozens of police assembled on an escalator at the mall.

"When unarmed #blacklivesmatter protesters showed up to peacefully protest at Mall Of America, this is a fraction of the police that showed up, dressed in militarized gear," Kweli wrote. "They secured the fuck out of that escalator."

For years, the shopping mall has been one of the many mirrors for how Americans see themselves. Sometimes the reflection is flattering, showing a portrait of success and even happiness. Other times it reveals a darker side, exposing greed, lifestyles of excess, and a national infatuation with material goods as a sign of status. As suburbia has aged, its utopic idyll has been altered. Cul-de-sacs, housing plans, and shopping malls are no longer perceived as safe harbors from the troubles of the world. Reality has finally caught up. Issues of race, class, and economics are now more prominent than ever in shopping malls and the suburban landscapes that rise and fall around them. Never has that been more evident than in recent times, particularly as the mall continues to be a flashpoint of unrest.

In December of 2016, on the day after Christmas, a rash of disturbances were reported at malls across America. In Fort Worth, Texas, police officer Tamara Valle responded to a fight that had broken out in the food court at Hulen Mall. Teenagers, more than 200, were running, screaming, and fighting. Stores went on lockdown, many with customers still inside. Hundreds of miles away, on the East Coast, similar scenes were unfolding at malls in Connecticut, New Jersey, and North Carolina.

At Beachwood Place in Cleveland, police responded to a fight involving some 500 people, mostly teenagers. As with similar scenes at other malls, shoppers flooded the promenades and sought shelter in storefronts. Videos uploaded to Facebook and Instagram documented the mayhem. Officers eventually used pepper spray to disperse the large crowds. Monroeville Mall also made news that night when fights broke out in the upper and lower levels. Witnesses reported that blood was visible on the floor where one of the altercations took place. Police arrested four youths following the disturbance.

That night, fights were reported at malls in at least a dozen states, including Illinois, Arizona, Indiana, and Colorado. Police departments across the country speculated that the fights may have been coordinated via social media, but cited that they had no evidence to confirm that theory. In the wake of the 2016 election, it would be so simple to blame the chaos as an outgrowth of the divisive rhetoric the nation has endured. Except that these disturbances have taken place for years. Following the most recent fights at Monroeville Mall, a shopkeeper who witnessed the incident may have said it best: "It's chaotic at the mall."

13 NEW FUTURES

It is better to live in a state of impermanence than in one of finality.
—GASTON BACHELARD, *THE POETICS OF SPACE*

An attractive young woman with long dark hair stands in the atrium of a shopping mall. She is alone. There are no other passersby—no shoppers or security guards or senior citizens walking laps. To her left is a seating area with two unoccupied chairs, one gray, the other wrapped in geometric-print fabric. Nearby an escalator operates without passengers. Its metal steps collapse and build and collapse again. Behind her the concourse is vacant. Brown, gray, and white floor tiles abut the terrazzo before vanishing in the distance. The outline of her body is silhouetted against a storefront of blue-white glass, giving the scene the impression of a half-rendered hologram. No merchandise or display racks are visible, and it's unclear if the store is out of business or sells nothing at all.

The woman, who is wearing a floral print dress that's cut just above the knee and white high heels that strap at the ankle, appears happy despite the loneliness of her surroundings. She is carrying four shopping bags. Two are slung over her right shoulder, while two more hang at her side. No store names appear on the bags, but each one is a different color. There is a sense she has been shopping for hours. With her shoulders turned and her eyes searching, the woman poses like a fashion model stopped at the end of a runway. Yet something is not right. She appears to be waiting for a photograph that will never be taken, and her expression seems to ask: *Can you see me?*

Step closer and the incongruities become more evident. The woman's face is blurred, almost pixelated—the way a .jpg looks when enlarged beyond its resolution. There is also a seam where her hair meets the background of the mall, and rough edges where the shopping bags float against storefront glass. Though from a distance she looked like a model that had stepped from the pages of a catalogue, up close her appearance is more that of a paper doll cut from a child's activity book. This woman is not real. She is an apparition, part of a floor-to-ceiling graphic affixed to a construction barrier that covers the entrance to a vacant storefront in Monroeville Mall, where the future is predicted in architectural renderings that dot the concourses.

The fictive shoppers in these renderings, more formally referred to as "people textures" and "populating images" in the vernacular of architects, are intended to give a sense of scale. For that reason, some architects even call them "scalies." But as their use in imagined spaces has grown over the years, so too have their roles. Author and futurist Geoff Manaugh has noted that architects often employ people textures as a subtle way to manipulate perception: "You can take the most random rendering and just stick in a few people—someone listening to an iPod, somebody reading a newspaper, maybe a couple holding hands, some guy playing an acoustic guitar. Suddenly it's meant to make the entire building beyond critique; it's already part of our city."[1]

Manaugh is not alone in his observations. British writer, artist, and technologist James Bridle has also taken note of the growing prevalence of these fictive people and what they represent. But he refers to them by another name. "The Render Ghosts are the people who live inside our imaginations, in the liminal space between the present and the future, the real and the virtual, the physical and the digital," Bridle writes.

A world of architecture, urbanism and the city before it is completed—which is also never. They inhabit a space which exists only in the virtual spaces of 3D computer rendering software, projected onto billboards, left to rot and torn down when the actual future arrives; never quite as glossy or as perfect as our renderings of it would like it to be, or have prepared us for.[2]

At Monroeville Mall the future is unclear, like the pixelated expression of the fictive young woman in the floral print dress. And she is not alone. Render ghosts haunt vacant storefronts throughout the mall, their presence, alongside phone numbers that encourage would-be retailers to inquire about leasing information, boasts of a more prosperous tomorrow. But whether that future comes remains to be seen. Render ghosts make such aspirations seem real, save for the uncanny valley, and offer a counterbalance to the fear of decay and perceived obsolescence.

As social and economic realities have threatened to disrupt the dream of the mall, however, there are fixers waiting in the wings—professionals versed in rehabilitation. Firms like KA Architecture are rendering the mall's next phase in its history. "With competition from open-air and mixed-use centers, enclosed malls sometimes struggle to maintain consumer interest," a company brochure states. "We work closely with developers to reinvent enclosed malls into vibrant hybrid centers, positioned to compete with the lifestyle centers in their markets."[3]

The mall is no longer a cultural phenomenon at its zenith, attracting hundreds of thousands of people who want nothing more than to experience what a mall has to offer. That moment came and went nearly thirty years ago. Today it's more of a cultural artifact either inching toward total obsolescence or poised for dramatic reinvention—whichever comes first.

"Malls are still cornerstones for a lot of the communities they serve," said Jesse Tron. "But we're coming to a point where we're going to have to drastically change our definitions." Tron, a spokesman for the International Council of Shopping

Centers, explained how public perception of the mall has changed. I called him because I was in search of the definitive voice of the mall, or as close an approximation as I could find. It was the equivalent of talking to a car salesman and asking if the automobile was still relevant. I knew the answer would be yes, but I wanted to hear what words he would choose. I wanted to know the story of the mall from the perspective of someone who analyzed its relevance each day.

"It goes back to the days of the Greek agora," Tron said. "People have always congregated around a central point of commerce." He noted how, for decades, the shopping mall quite dutifully fulfilled that need for the buying public. It was a central hub for the purchase of goods, and it also provided a social experience. That is, until the advent of the internet and the popularity of online shopping decentralized the whole industry—transforming once-vibrant centers into ghost malls, pushing others to the verge of bankruptcy. But after more than a decade of decline and closures, there are still 1,222 shopping malls across America, and Tron is hopeful that number will hold.

"What's old is new again," he said. "We're now in a period where we are reverting to more of that community-based, experiential, entertainment-focused kind of shopping center." In other words, malls with places to sit and relax, recharge your phone, watch a movie, eat dinner. It's a return to the social elements that defined the malls that Victor Gruen designed. But it also begs the question: Do people still want to do those things in a shopping mall?

On the lower level of Monroeville Mall, where the twin escalators meet, there is a bronze bust of a man named Harry Soffer. Mounted on a marble column, it includes an inscription: "A man whose vision and foresight made all that you see here possible." Soffer is one of the men who developed this mall. A man who took a crater in the earth that was once a strip mine and transformed it into a gleaming, enclosed metropolis. If he were a science fiction or fantasy author, he would be lauded for his skill as a world-builder—his ability to construct a place that has stood for nearly half a century.

The shopping mall is, in its own right, a paracosm; a term used by psychologists to describe an imaginary world. These worlds have their own geography, history, and languages, and continue to grow over a period of months, years, or even decades. Children who are creative often build paracosms—not only for expression but also for escape. Writers do too. J.R.R. Tolkien's Middle-earth, with its myriad species, histories, and landscapes, is one example. Henry Darger's *Realms of the Unreal*, which the writer and artist began creating as a child, is another. In the utopic world of the shopping mall, Victor Gruen is its omnipotent creator.

As the shopping mall evolves, it no longer resembles the place crystallized in my memory. Which begs more questions than it answers: Am I simply a render ghost inhabiting Victor Gruen's imagined world? Are we all apparitions strolling in the faded hallways of his failed dream? If you follow the lifecycle of an architectural fantasy like Southdale Center in Edina, Minnesota, there is a definitive fiction at play. There is what Gruen imagined the mall could be, and there is what it became. The distinction between the two is important, because when Gruen washed his hands of the mall late in life, he did so because he lost control of the world he had built. And not only control of the way other architects and developers interpreted and later bastardized his concept, but control of the narrative he wished to tell. Shopping malls were no longer "Tomorrow's main street, today," they were harbingers of consumerism's dominance over human behavior, marring the very suburban landscape that Gruen wished to transform.

At Monroeville Mall, as I stand in an empty end court, I feel distant from the landscape around me. It is the same space where, as a young boy, I watched in amazement as the Clock of Nations came alive each hour, its animatronic puppets celebrating the passage of time with a song. It is also the same courtyard where Gimbels department store once opened onto the mall, and where I gushed with joy each time I crossed that threshold, which meant I was stepping into another world. On weekends, it's where I sat with my father in the shadow of the clock tower, waiting for my mother to finish her shift at the Gimbels service desk so we could all be together again. And at Christmas and Easter, it's where I rode the holiday train, waving to my parents as I circled the courtyard.

But none of that feels real anymore. If anything, it reminds me of a dream degraded by the passage of time. Where the mall is a place on a map, and a wellspring of memory. Where aspiration and reality collide. Where discord gives way to violence. Where material desires test impulse control. Where past, present, and future are simultaneously collapsed. Where all but the most salient details are lost in the ether. My mother's smile as she takes my hand and we walk. The smell of the pine-tree air freshener in my father's blue Caprice. The rainbow neon in the food court and how bright it glowed. The black infinity of the video arcade and the tinny clang of quarters in coin slots. My sister's roller skates and the sound of the wheels rolling on smooth concrete. Friday nights when the concourses came alive and thousands of people flooded through the doors. Darkened hallways and storefront security gates rolled down at closing time. It is the mall rendered in spare parts pulled from memory, its image flickering like a hologram, threatening to vanish before the future ever arrives.

ACKNOWLEDGMENTS

I am indebted to my editors, Ian Bogost and Christopher Schaberg, whose insightful feedback helped me to shape and refine this book. My gratefulness to Haaris Naqvi at Bloomsbury for always thoughtfully keeping me on track. To Yona Harvey, whose support of my writing has been a gift. I am thankful to Susan Clements for her thoughtful comments and keen eyes, and for encouraging me to originally submit my proposal. Thank you to Katie Reilly for being a good friend, listener, and supporter, and to Norene Walworth for her wise counsel.

To my parents, Vikki and Tom Newton, I am grateful for their lifelong support of my ideas, and for always encouraging my decision to pursue a field with no guarantees but invaluable rewards. To my sister, Jennifer Newton Shuttleworth, who has always believed in me even when I didn't believe in myself.

And most of all, my love and gratitude to my wife Michelle, whose compassion and generosity continually astounds me, and my sons Ethan and Nico, whose joy and curiosity about the world gives me hope for the future.

NOTES

Prologue

1   "A Break-Through for Two-Level Shopping Centers,"
    Architectural Forum 105 (December 1956): 114–26.

2   Ben Welter, "Nov. 28, 1956: Frank Lloyd Wright at Southdale,"
    Star Tribune, November 28, 2015, accessed February 29, 2016,
    http://www.startribune.com/nov-28-1956-frank-lloyd-wright-
    at-southdale/126070188/.

3   Jeff Baenen, "Indoor Shopping Mall is 30 Years Old," *Times-
    News*, October 8, 1986, 10.

4   "The Splashiest Shopping Center in the U.S.," *Life*, December
    10, 1956, 61–66.

5   Victor Gruen and Larry Smith, *Shopping Towns USA: The
    Planning of Shopping Centers* (New York: Van Nostrand
    Reinhold, 1960), 22–24.

6   Malcolm Gladwell, "The Terrazzo Jungle," *New Yorker*, March
    15, 2004, http://www.newyorker.com/magazine/2004/03/15/
    the-terrazzo-jungle.

7   Victor Gruen, *The Heart of Our Cities: The Urban Crisis:
    Diagnosis and Cure* (New York: Simon and Schuster, 1964),
    194–95.

Chapter 2

1   Stefan Lorant, *Pittsburgh: The Story of an American City* (New York: Doubleday & Company, 1964).

2   Rami El Samahy, "Robert Pease: The Man Who Helped Remake Postwar Pittsburgh," *Storyboard*, March 30, 2016, accessed April 6, 2016, http://blog.cmoa.org/2016/03/bob-pease-the-man-who-helped-remake-postwar-pittsburgh/.

3   Eileen Foley, "For Monroeville the Bloom Is Not Off the 30-Year Boom," *Pittsburgh Post-Gazette*, March 20, 1980, East edition, 1, 3.

4   Burt Bacharach (1970), "Everybody's Out of Town," [Recorded by B.J. Thomas]. On *Everybody's Out of Town* [LP].

5   Eleanor Chute, "Mall at 25 Holding Its Own," *Pittsburgh Post-Gazette*, August 11, 1994, E-11.

6   Louis A. Chandler, *A History of Patton Township*, Monroeville Historical Society, September, 2012, http://monroevillehistorical.org/component/jifile/download/N2E0OTUxMDI0YjhjYTA3NTVjY2ZhNTNiNTZmM2NmNTU=/history-of-patton-township-pdf.

7   "The South Hills Village Opens in Great Style," *Pittsburgh Post-Gazette*, July 29, 1965.

8   Torsten Ove, "The Next Page: Michael James Genovese—The Life & Times of the Last Great Pittsburgh Mobster," *Pittsburgh Post-Gazette*, April 19, 2009, accessed May 16, 2016, http://www.post-gazette.com/Op-Ed/2009/04/19/The-Next-Page-Michael-James-Genovese-The-life-times-of-the-last-great-Pittsburgh-mobster/stories/200904190162.

9 Jeff Baenen, "First Shopping Center Celebrates Its 30th Year," *Dispatch*, October 9, 1986, 22.

10 "Mall was Built for Lazy Shoppers," *Pittsburgh Post-Gazette*, May 14, 1969, 32, accessed 6, 2016, https://news.google.com/newspapers?id=HNpaAAAAIBAJ&sjid=1GwDAAAAIBAJ&pg=2348%2C2443445.

11 Advertisement cited in text: *Pittsburgh Press*, May 12, 1969, 53, https://news.google.com/newspapers?id=ge4iAAAAIBAJ&sjid=G1AEAAAAIBAJ&pg=5870%2C5849116.

12 John Little, "Monroeville Mall Ministry—Proposed Mission in the Field," *Pittsburgh Press*, February 7, 1970, accessed April 6, 2016, https://news.google.com/newspapers?nid=1144&dat=19700207&id=Vc8bAAAAIBAJ&sjid=z1AEAAAAIBAJ&pg=7245,2445612&hl=en.

13 "Big Time Shopping," television commercial for Monroeville Mall, https://www.youtube.com/watch?v=_bofJwKnGNA.

14 Advertisement cited in text: *Pittsburgh Post-Gazette*, May 14, 1969, 29, accessed 6, 2016, https://news.google.com/newspapers?nid=gL9scSG3K_gC&dat=19690514&printsec=frontpage&hl=en.

Chapter 4

1 Nick Freand Jones, interview with George A. Romero, *Forbidden*, BBC Two, February 2, 1997, https://www.youtube.com/watch?v=c2c0ADotCR0.

2 M. Jeffrey Hardwick, *Mall Maker: Victor Gruen, Architect of an American Dream* (Philadelphia: University of Pennsylvania Press, 2004), 2.

3 Norman M. Klein, *The Vatican to Vegas: A History of Special Effects* (New York: New Press, 2004), 338

4 Giandomenico Amendola, "Urban Mindscapes Reflected in Shop Windows," in *Urban Mindscapes of Europe*, eds. Godela Weiss-Sussex and Franco Bianchini Rodopi (Amsterdam: Editions Rodopi BV, 2006), 91.

5 *True Stories*. Directed by David Byrne (Los Angeles: Warner Bros., 1986), https://www.youtube.com/watch?v=4cYYPpZ8rFI.

Chapter 7

1 Kathryn H. Anthony, "The Shopping Mall: A Teenage Hangout," *Adolescence* 78 (Summer 1985): 307–11.

2 Steven R. Churm, "Tiffany will hang out all summer in shopping malls and try to meet new friends," *Los Angeles Times*, July 2, 1987, accessed October 26, 2016, http://articles.latimes.com/1987-07-02/news/hl-1724_1_shopping-malls.

3 William Severini Kowinski, *The Malling of America: An Inside Look at the Great Consumer Paradise* (New York: William Morrow and Company, Inc., 1985), 48.

Chapter 10

1 Rachel Carson, *The Sense of Wonder* (New York: Harper & Row, 1987), 42.

Chapter 11

1 Matt Stopera, "Completely Surreal Photos of America's Abandoned Malls," *BuzzFeed*, April 2, 2014, accessed June 7, 2014, https://www.buzzfeed.com/mjs538/completely-surreal-pictures-of-americas-abandoned-malls.

Chapter 13

1 Rob Walker, "Go Figure," *New York Times Magazine*, February 4, 2011, accessed October 7, 2016, http://www.nytimes.com/2011/02/06/magazine/06fob-consumed-t.html.

2 James Bridle, "The Render Ghosts," *Electronic Voice Phenomena*, November 14, 2013, accessed May 3, 2016, http://www.electronicvoicephenomena.net/index.php/the-render-ghosts-james-bridle/.

3 KA Architecture brochure, http://www.kainc.com/downloads/ka_aquisition_040709.pdf.

INDEX

Adams, Robert   125
Adan, Dahir A.   131
AIDS   81
Akron, Ohio   122–4
Ala Moana Nails   14
Allegheny Center Mall,
    Pittsburgh,
    Pennsylvania   41
Allegheny Conference
    on Economic
    Development   39
Al Shabaab   131
Amendola, Giandomenico   59
America is Dead
    (Christof)   124–5
American Rust Belt   123, 126
Anthony, Kathryn H.   82
    "The Shopping Mall: A
    Teenage Hangout"   82
Anthrax   70
Architectural Forum   6
architecture, *see* suburban-
    urban retail
Arizona   134

B. Dalton Bookseller   11, 28
Bachelard, Gaston   135
    The Poetics of Space   135
Baker, Faith Hall   121
Banana Republic   14
Barney Miller (TV series)   29
Bath & Body Works   116
BBC   57–8
Beachwood Place, Cleveland,
    Ohio   134
Belk   34
Bergen Mall, Paramus, New
    Jersey   83
Berry, Wendell   119
Bertoia, Harry   6, 13
    Golden Trees   6, 13
*Bill and Ted's Excellent
    Adventure* (Herek)   84
Bird, Larry   72
Black, Clint   106
Black Lives Matter   129, 132
Blood, Bread, and Poetry
    (Rich)   1
Bloomingdale's   34

Blues Brothers, The (Landis)   85
Boscov's   118
Braddock, Pennsylvania   41
Branigan, Laura   117
Bridle, James   137
Britain   18
Brooks, Garth   106
Brown, Michael   129
Brown Derby   28
Burger King   75
BuzzFeed   122
Byrne, David   60–2
   True Stories   60–2, 84

California   2
Camp Beverly Hills   79
Canton Centre Mall, Canton,
   Ohio   125, 126
Caribou Coffee   14
Carnegie Mellon
   University   105, 108
Carson, Rachel   115
Cascade Mall, Burlington,
   Washington   132
Cetin, Arcan   132
chain stores   14, 27
Chicago, Illinois   38, 43
Chicago Bulls   73
Chopping Mall (Wynorski)   84
Chopra, Joyce
   Smooth Talk   84
Christof, Tag   124–5
   America is Dead   124–5

Cinnabon   9
Circus (magazine)   96
civil rights era   57
Clark, Jamar   132
Cleveland, Ohio   38, 130
Cloverleaf Mall, Chesterfield,
   Virginia   126
Coach   14
Cold War   81
Colorado   131, 134
Colors by Benetton   79
Columbine High School
   massacre   131
Commando (Lester)   83
Conley's Motor Inn   90–1
Connecticut   134
consumerism   4, 6, 16, 27,
   46, 57–62, 68, 69, 70–7,
   79–81, 82, 85–7, 96, 115,
   133, 139, 141
Contempo   103
Coronado Mall, Albuquerque,
   New Mexico   124
Crestwood Mall, St. Louis,
   Missouri   126
Crossroads Center, St. Cloud,
   Minnesota   131–2
Crowe, Cameron   84

Darger, Henry   140
   Realms of the Unreal   140
Dark Knight Returns, The
   (Miller)   96

Dark Knight Rises, The
    (Nolan) 131
Dawn of the Dead
    (Romero) 16, 57, 59,
    115–16
Dayton's 5, 7
Deadmalls.com 121
Def Leppard 73, 75
   Pyromania 75
Del Amo Fashion Center,
    Torrance, California 45
Dern, Laura 84
Detroit, Michigan 5, 38
Die Hard (McTiernan) 92
Di Pomodoro 28
Dixie Square Mall, Harvey,
    Illinois 27, 85, 126
Dobler, Bruce 70
Dollar Savings Bank 86
Donaldson's 7
Don-Mark Realty 38, 47–8
Dragon City Accupressure 14
drug use 38, 65, 67,
    81, 131
Duncan, John J. 48
Dungeons & Dragons 96

East Africa 131
Eastland Mall, North Versailles,
    Pennsylvania 44
Eat 'Em and Smile (Roth) 75
Eberhardt, Thom
   Night of the Comet 83

Edina, Minnesota 1, 4, 12,
    27, 44
Euclid Square Mall, Euclid,
    Ohio 126
Europe 5, 5, 59

Facebook 121, 134
Fast Times at Ridgemont High
    (Heckerling) 84–5
Ferguson, Missouri 129
Flashdance (Lyne) 117
Fleer 75
Foot Locker 116
Fortune 7

G. C. Murphy 51, 73, 120
Gap 103
Garlits, Don 53
Garner, Eric 129–30
Genovese, Michael 44
ghost malls 119–26, 139
Gillette, Guy 12, 14
Gimbels 25, 26–7, 28, 30–6,
    48, 56, 118, 141
Gladwell, Malcolm 16
Golack, Kim Jo 121
Golden Trees (Bertoia) 6, 13
Great Recession 123, 131
Greengate Mall, Greensburg,
    Pennsylvania 41, 72–7,
    85–6, 119, 126
Greengate Mall Revisited
    (website) 121

Greensburg,
      Pennsylvania   85, 119
Gruen, Victor   5–9, 11, 12, 13,
      15–19, 58, 120, 130, 139,
      140, 141
Gruen Transfer/Gruen
      Effect   58, 59
Guns N' Roses   76
Guttman, Herman   8

H&M   14
Hard Rock Café   75
Harrisburg, Pennsylvania   56
Hawthorne Plaza Mall,
      Hawthorne,
      California   126
Heavy Metal
      (magazine)   74, 75
Heckerling, Amy
   *Fast Times at Ridgemont
      High*   84–5
Herek, Stephen
   *Bill and Ted's Excellent
      Adventure*   84
Holiday Inn   107, 108
Holmes, James   131
Hot Topic   116
Howard, Ebenezer   18
Huey Lewis and the News   68
Hughes, John
   Weird Science   83
Hulen Mall, Fort Worth,
      Texas   133

IKEA   19
Illinois   2, 134
Indiana   134
Indiana University of
      Pennsylvania   103
Instagram   129, 133, 134
International Council of
      Shopping Centers   138
*Interpretation of Ordinary
      Landscapes, The*
      (Lewis)   37
Invasion U.S.A. (Zito)   84

J. C. Penney   29, 95
J. Crew   14
Jacobs, Jane   39
Johnson, Magic   72
Jones, Davon   127, 128
Jordan, Michael   72
Joseph Horne Company   28,
      48, 97, 102

KA Architecture   138
Kansas City Chiefs   129
Kaufmann's   34, 103
Kavanaugh, Gere   46
Kinkade, Thomas   116
kiosk   9, 14, 117
Klein, Norman M.   58
Kmart   118
Kowinski, William
      Severini   45, 86
Kweli, Talib   133

Labelscar.com   60
Landis, John
    The Blues Brothers   85
Laurel Highlands,
        Pennsylvania   113, 120
Lawrence, David L.   39
Lebowitz, Eugene   38, 48
Leeds, Herbert A.   48
Lemonheads   105
Lester, Mark L.
    Commando   83
Lewis, Edward J.   38, 48
Lewis, Peirce F.   37
    *The Interpretation of
        Ordinary Landscapes*   37
Life   7, 12
Liz Claiborne   79
Lorant, Stefan   39
    *Pittsburgh: The Story of An
        American City*   39
Los Angeles Times   83
Lyne, Adrian
    Flashdance   117

McDonald, Sheri   121
McTiernan, John
    Die Hard   92
Macy's   8, 9, 19, 20, 34, 113,
        127, 129
Mall of America, Bloomington,
        Minnesota   4, 21, 131,
        132-3
Manaugh, Geoff   137

Mangione, Chuck   113
Maryvale Shopping City,
        Phoenix, Arizona   44-5
Mason, Mark E.   38, 48
Megadeth   70, 95
Mellon, Richard King   39
Metal Maniacs (magazine)   96
Midland Mall, Warwick, Rhode
        Island   27
Miller, Frank   96
    The Dark Knight Returns   96
Milton Bradley   80-1
    Mall Madness (board
        game)   80-1
Minneapolis, Minnesota   1, 3,
        4, 132
Miracle Mile Shopping
        Center, Monroeville,
        Pennsylvania   44, 88-93
modernism   15, 39, 120
Monroeville,
        Pennsylvania   40, 42,
        43-4, 45, 48, 55, 92, 106,
        127-9
Monroeville Mall, Monroeville,
        Pennsylvania   27, 38,
        42, 43, 45-8, 54, 57-8,
        65, 113-18, 115, 127-30,
        134, 135-6, 137-8,
        139-40, 141
    Clock of Nations   28, 46,
        117-18, 141
    Ice Palace   23, 48, 117

Montgomery Ward   121
Moore, Alan   96
  Watchmen   96
Morrissey   105
Moses, Robert   39
Motley Crüe   71
Motörhead   70
MTV   83
  Museum of UnNatural
    History   83
Mumford, Lewis   39
Muzak   9, 95, 113

National Record Mart   11, 75,
    86, 120
NBA Hoops   75
Nelson, Gary   119–20
New Jersey   2, 134
Newsweek   7
New York City   43
New York Times   7
Night of the Comet
    (Eberhardt)   83
Night of the Living Dead
    (Romero)   57
Nolan, Christopher
  The Dark Knight Rises   131
Norris, Chuck   84
North Carolina   134
Northland Center, Southfield,
    Michigan   5
North Towne Square Mall,
    Toledo, Ohio   126

Northway Mall, Ross Township,
    Pennsylvania   41
Nuclear Assault   95

Oakland, California   38
Oasis   11
Oates, Joyce Carol   84
OU812 (Van Halen)   75

paracosm   140
Paul, Rev. William M.   47
Pease, Robert   39–40
Penn-Lincoln Parkway   44
Pennsylvania Turnpike   38,
    44, 56, 67, 71, 72, 93, 106
Perkins, Anthony
  Psycho III   71
Philadelphia, Pennsylvania   56
Pier I Imports   70
Pittsburgh, Pennsylvania   8,
    10, 25, 27, 28, 37, 38,
    39–48, 47, 93, 95, 120
*Pittsburgh: The Story of
    An American City*
    (Lorant)   39
Pittsburgh Pirates   25–6, 34
Pittsburgh Press   46
Pivirotto, Richard R.   48
Plum, Pennsylvania   65–9
Poetics of Space, The
    (Bachelard)   135
Proactiv   117
Pryor, Terrelle   129